CW01506840

FOOLPROOF

• BATCH COOKING •

60 SIMPLE MEALS TO SAVE YOU
MONEY, TIME AND EFFORT

KATIE MARSHALL

PHOTOGRAPHY BY
RITA PLATTS

Quadrille

Quadrille, Penguin Random House UK,
One Embassy Gardens, 8 Viaduct Gardens,
London SW11 7BW

Quadrille Publishing Limited is part of
the Penguin Random House group of
companies whose addresses can be found
at global.penguinrandomhouse.com

Copyright © Quadrille 2025
Photography © Rita Platts 2025
Design © Quadrille 2025

Penguin Random House values and
supports copyright. Copyright fuels
creativity, encourages diverse voices,
promotes freedom of expression and
supports a vibrant culture. Thank you
for purchasing an authorized edition of
this book and for respecting intellectual
property laws by not reproducing, scanning
or distributing any part of it by any means
without permission. You are supporting
authors and enabling Penguin Random
House to continue to publish books for
everyone. No part of this book may be
used or reproduced in any manner for the
purpose of training artificial intelligence
technologies or systems. In accordance with
Article 4(3) of the DSM Directive 2019/790,
Penguin Random House expressly reserves
this work from the text and data mining
exception.

Published by Quadrille in 2025

www.penguin.co.uk

A CIP catalogue record for this book is
available from the British Library

ISBN 9781837834969
10 9 8 7 6 5 4 3 2 1

Colour reproduction by p2d

Printed in China by C&C Offset Printing Co., Ltd.

The authorised representative in the EEA
is Penguin Random House Ireland, Morrison
Chambers, 32 Nassau Street, Dublin
D02 YH68.

Penguin Random House is committed to
a sustainable future for our business, our
readers and our planet. This book is made
from Forest Stewardship Council® certified
paper.

Managing Director
Sarah Lavelle

Editor
Sofie Shearman

Series Designer
Emily Lapworth

Designer
Katy Everett

Photographer
Rita Platts

Food Stylist
Katie Marshall

Food Stylist Assistants
Jessica Geddes, Caitlin Macdonald
and Maria Gurevich

Prop Stylist
Max Robinson

Head of Production
Stephen Lang

Production Controller
Sumayyah Waheed

CONTENTS

Introduction 4

One Cook, Two Meals 6

Hearty Soups 28

Traybakes 46

Winter Warmers 62

Meaty Mains 78

Summer Staples 94

Freezer Fillers 108

Preserves 130

Index 142

Acknowledgements 144

INTRODUCTION

Batch cooking is, as a concept, aspirational. It encapsulates the person who thinks ahead, meal-plans, prepares. Has a tidy freezer! I would have generally put myself in a more 'haphazard' category than that – enjoying ad-libbing meals and seeing what I fancy eating, day by day. But I've realized that I have the knack to batch cook by nature. I grew up in a family of six, where most meals were prepared in a 30cm (12in) casserole dish. This allowed for a generous dinner and then leftovers (which were usually enjoyed as lunches later in the week).

It's my thinking that if you're chopping one onion, you might as well chop three. You just upsize your cookware for a bigger surface area and the larger quantity will cook in the same time as the solo onion. It's not much more effort to upscale a recipe and it is exponentially rewarding to eat the fruits of your labour several times more after that initial energy drive. One cook equals many delicious meals!

In the main, this book contains recipes that make eight portions, to do with as you will. I see batch cooking as preparing a massive vat or tray or something – to feed a hungry rabble, or for a dinner for four for two nights in a row. You could eat a couple of portions 'fresh' then portion out the rest to have later that week, or freeze for another time. And then, when you have a variety of dinners lined up in your freezer, you're basically perusing an aisle of ready meals when you're debating what to eat the next day. As a working mum, I love to be able to conjure something from the freezer (for kids or adults) and know that at some point in the past (pinpointed if I remember to label my containers), I made something from scratch to feed and nourish my family.

Filling your freezer

My dedicated freezer fillers chapter (page 108) is advance prep for those lazy/busy days when you don't have the mental energy to forage in the local shop – cue a pre-made (by you) fishcake happily bronzing away in the oven while you get on with some work. And you never know when there might be an 'emergency' situation when you need to whip out freshly baked cookies!

Beyond this, a big proportion of the recipes in this book will lend themselves to freezing – either the final resting place for that leftover portion, or potentially the whole result of your batch cook. Some dishes I recommend freezing whole, unfinished (like the Fish Pie on page 48), or completely uncooked (like the Sausage Rolls on page 117). I would always recommend clearly labelling anything frozen with the recipe name, date of freezing and quantity of portions. It might seem over the top, but it could prove to be a lifesaver if you have a note of exactly what is in your freezer (on a piece of paper attached to the freezer door, or on a board in the kitchen). This will avoid defrosting the wrong thing – or finding something vintage in the back of the freezer that could have been perfectly delectable, if you'd only remembered it sooner.

The meals will remain at their optimum for up to three months and will be safe to eat beyond that, but the quality and colour will have started to deteriorate.

The texture of some foodstuffs, like pasta or potatoes, will be changed slightly by the science of freezing and defrosting, but I think it's a small price to pay for them being so conveniently available.

You must always cool food to room temperature before freezing, so that it doesn't raise the temperature of your freezer, or get condensation on it which will freeze as ice.

And always ensure that no sharp objects will pierce a bag of soup or curry!

One cook, two meals

My 'One Cook, Two Meals' chapter is a way of making your prep stretch further. The love and effort that goes into a slow-cooked Beef Shin Ragù (see page 9) can then convert to a Lasagne (see page 11) — a famously labour-intensive dish that has had one of the components taken care of in advance. This book is about trying to be clever and logical with your time, to make mealtimes run more smoothly in the future.

Cooking for a crowd

Even though I'm a trained chef, and sometimes spend five days out of seven cooking eight recipes a day, I always feel completely flummoxed when it comes to cooking for a crowd — but I think I've cracked it with a good chunk of these recipes. There are dishes that simmer and soften in the oven for hours, others that bubble on the stove in far less time — but all are, as the name suggests, foolproof — and suitable for midweek meals, or some weekend hosting. My mother-in-law is the queen of batch cooking for the festive season. In advance of having the wider family come to stay, she will have almost every meal cooked, labelled and frozen, leaving more time to enjoy the company. It really is a stress-buster.

Useful items

- I still always prefer cooking in a large, cast-iron pan — not only for the nostalgia, but also to reduce the risk of burning that accompanies longer cooking times.

- A metal funnel is very helpful for decanting preserves — and usually dishwasher-friendly, to boot.

- To minimize the chance of freezer burn, it's important to store food in airtight containers or sealed bags. Plastic tubs, freezer bags and old takeaway containers are all useful for portioning up.

- Silicone moulds are great for freezing up portions and come in all shapes and sizes. When frozen, you can ease the portions from their containers and transfer to freezer bags to stack more space-efficiently. This also works for open-freezing — where food items are frozen on a lined, flat tray (such as on pages 117 and 113), then moved to a freezer bag once fully hardened. A tip I learned from my partner is to freeze child-size portions in the holes of muffin tins, carefully removing them and popping them into airtight bags once fully frozen.

- I love using glass storage containers for portioning up meals for the week. They're a stylish and microwave-friendly way to prep office lunches, and they stack nicely, too! Being aesthetically pleasing, they're also a welcome addition to the dining table so they save on washing up. You can buy sets online that sometimes contain various sizes, so cater for different quantities (and appetites).

Reheating

To prepare from frozen, either defrost food overnight in the fridge (never defrost at room temperature or you risk bacterial growth) or using the appropriate microwave setting. Food should then be reheated until piping hot all the way through. Once food has been reheated, dispose of any leftovers — reheating for a second time after cooling can increase the chances of bacteria.

ONE COOK, TWO MEALS

How to upgrade your leftovers! These recipes intentionally make double provisions so that you have two completely different meals from one root recipe — a surefire way to avoid that meal-planning monotony.

BEEF SHIN RAGÙ

This ragù is so rich and delicious, made extra special by slow-cooking the meat with lots of red wine and aromatic herbs. It's a great one to upscale slightly so you have enough left over to make a lasagne, as you won't want this dish to end! The parmesan and butter stirred through at the end is the secret to making it ultra glossy and decadent.

6 tbsp olive oil
4 carrots, peeled and finely diced
4 celery sticks, finely chopped
3 onions, finely chopped
5 garlic cloves, crushed
1.2kg (2lb 10oz) beef shin (shank), cut into rough 2.5cm (1in) chunks
5 tbsp tomato purée (paste)
500ml (2 cups) red wine
700ml (2¾ cups) beef stock (made with two stock pots, if using)
1 x 400g (14oz) tin (can) chopped tomatoes
4 sprigs of rosemary
4 bay leaves
1 tbsp caster (superfine) sugar
50g (2oz) salted butter
50g (2oz) grated parmesan, plus extra to serve
salt and freshly ground black pepper
pappardelle or polenta, to serve

Preheat the oven to 180°C/160°C fan/350°F/Gas 4.

Heat 2 tablespoons of olive oil in a large casserole dish over a medium heat and cook the carrots, celery and onions for 10–12 minutes, until softened. Add the garlic and fry for another minute, then remove the veg to a bowl. Increase the heat and add another 2 tablespoons of olive oil. Fry the beef shin until browned (do this in two batches, removing to a bowl when browned), seasoning with salt and pepper as you go. Use the remaining oil for the second batch.

When all the meat is browned, add back to the pan along with the softened vegetables. Add the tomato purée and fry for a minute before adding the wine. Bring to the boil then add the stock, tomatoes, rosemary, bay leaves and sugar. Cover with the lid and place in the oven for 2 hours, then take out of the oven and remove the lid. Return to the oven and continue to cook, uncovered, for another 30 minutes.

Remove the rosemary and bay leaves. Shred the meat by mashing or pulling with a fork, then stir through the butter and parmesan. Serve half with the pappardelle or polenta (and plenty of extra parmesan) and reserve the rest for the Lasagne (see page 11).

Serves 4, with leftovers for lasagne
—
Prep 15 mins
—
Cook 3 hours

LASAGNE

I can never bear to make a lasagne from scratch because I get in a pickle with the different components – but repurposing some ragù (especially a slow-cooked Beef Shin Ragù – see page 9) takes one task off your hands. My ratios of sauce to pasta mean that this is a super rich and really juicy dish – best enjoyed when you need some real comfort food.

1 x quantity of leftover Beef Shin Ragù (see page 9)
1 x 400g (14oz) tin (can) chopped tomatoes
2 tbsp tomato purée (paste)
75g (2½oz) salted butter
75g (2½oz) plain (all-purpose) flour
700ml (2¾ cups) whole milk
250g (9oz) mature cheddar
2 tsp dijon mustard
150g (5½oz) dried lasagne sheets
salt and freshly ground black pepper

To serve (optional)
salad
garlic bread (see page 114)

Preheat the oven to 200°C/180°C fan/400°F/Gas 6.

To start, put the leftover ragù into a saucepan along with the chopped tomatoes and tomato purée. Simmer for 10 minutes while you prepare the white sauce.

For the béchamel, melt the butter in a medium saucepan over a medium heat. Add the flour and use a balloon whisk to mix to a paste. Slowly add the milk in increments, whisking well between additions to make a nice smooth sauce. When all the milk has been added, increase the heat and let bubble for 1–2 minutes, until thickened. Remove from the heat and season with salt and pepper. Add half the cheddar and all of the mustard. Mix to combine.

Put one third of the ragù into the base of a roughly 25 x 35cm (10 x 14in) ovenproof dish. Spoon one quarter of the white sauce on top and sprinkle with some cheddar. Arrange one layer of lasagne sheets on top (breaking up the sheets to fill the gaps, if needed). Spoon in another third of the ragù and then another drizzle of the white sauce, sprinkling with some cheddar. Place another layer of lasagne sheets on top, then the remaining ragù and remaining white sauce. Finish with the remaining cheddar.

Bake in the oven for 40–45 minutes, until golden and bubbling. Let it stand for 10 minutes to cool down a little, before serving with a green side salad and some garlic bread, if liked.

Serves 4–6
–
Prep 15 mins
–
Cook 1 hour

BOLOGNAISE

Bolognaise is the ultimate batch cook to me – it was made to be simmered away in a big pan, making the house smell deliciously sweet and fragrant. This could easily be prepped to feed a crowd of eight, but here I've done a big batch so that half can magically moonlight as Chilli con Carne (see overleaf), meaning one lot of frying and lovingly stirring makes two deliciously different meals.

3 tbsp olive oil
2 onions, finely chopped
3 celery sticks, finely chopped
3 carrots, peeled and finely diced
3 garlic cloves, crushed
750g (1lb 10oz) minced (ground) beef
3 tbsp tomato purée (paste)
1 tbsp caster (superfine) sugar
200ml (generous ¾ cup) red wine
680g (1lb 8oz) jar passata (strained tomatoes)
300ml (1¼ cups) water mixed with 1 x beef stock pot
2 bay leaves

To serve
spaghetti
grated parmesan

Put a large casserole dish over a low–medium heat. Add 2 tablespoons of olive oil and then the onions, celery and carrots and cook for 10–12 minutes. Add the garlic and fry for another minute, then remove the veg to a bowl.

Add the remaining 1 tablespoon of olive oil and increase the heat a little to medium–high. Add the beef mince and pan fry for 8–10 minutes until browned all over, breaking up the chunks with a wooden spoon. Add the tomato purée and sugar and fry for another minute, then add the wine. Bring to a bubble before adding the passata and stock, and returning the vegetables to the pan. Add the bay leaves then bring to the boil. Reduce to a simmer and cook for 20–25 minutes. Remove the bay leaves then set aside 700g (1lb 9oz) to make a chilli. Serve with spaghetti and plenty of grated parmesan.

Serves 4, with leftovers for chilli
–
Prep 15 mins
–
Cook 50 mins

One Cook, Two Meals

CHILLI CON CARNE

This meal takes as long to whip up as it does to boil the rice to go alongside it! Adding plenty of aromatic spices means that your leftovers seamlessly transition from their bolognaise past into an entirely new meal. If you're not a fan of kidney beans, try using mixed beans, chickpeas or even lentils.

1 tbsp olive oil
2 red (bell) peppers, cut into roughly
    1.5cm (½in) cubes
2 garlic cloves, crushed
1½ tsp chilli flakes
1½ tsp cumin seeds
1 tsp ground coriander
1 tsp ground cinnamon
700g (1lb 9oz) leftover Bolognaise
    (see page 13)
1 x 400g (14oz) tin (can) kidney beans,
    drained and rinsed
200ml (generous ¾ cup) beef stock
1 tbsp tomato purée (paste)

To serve
steamed rice
soured cream
guacamole
10g (¼oz) coriander (cilantro),
    roughly chopped

Heat the olive oil in a medium saucepan and then add the peppers. Fry over a medium–high heat for 5 minutes, until softened and starting to char a little. Add the garlic and cook for 30 seconds, then add the spices. Cook for a further 30 seconds before stirring through the bolognaise, kidney beans, beef stock and tomato purée. Simmer for 10 minutes before serving with rice, soured cream and guacamole, with coriander scattered over the top.

Serves 4
—
Prep 5 mins
—
Cook 16 mins

ROAST CHICKEN WITH LEMON, OLIVES AND NEW POTATOES

This is a roast chicken dinner – the lighter edition! I love a roasted new potato and these combine the joy of a crispy top and a juicy bottom, cooking in the chicken's juices. The slowly cooked lemon starts to caramelize and loses the sharp acidity it has when fresh.

1 x 1.8kg (4lb) free-range whole chicken
3 tbsp olive oil
2 lemons, ½ for stuffing and the
   remaining 1½ cut into wedges
1kg (2lb 2oz) baby potatoes,
   larger ones halved
340g (12oz) pitted green olives
   (drained weight)
6 garlic cloves, skin on and lightly
   bruised
30g (1oz) salted butter
200g (7oz) baby spinach
salt and freshly ground black pepper

Preheat the oven to 220°C/200°C fan/425°F/Gas 7. Rub the chicken all over with 1 tablespoon of olive oil and season with salt and pepper (inside and out). Put half a lemon into the chicken's cavity then place, breast-side down, into a baking dish (mine was approximately 30 x 35cm/12 x 14in). Place in the oven and roast for 20 minutes. Meanwhile, add the potatoes, olives, lemon wedges and garlic to a bowl and toss together with the remaining olive oil. Turn the chicken upside down (breast-side up) and scatter the potatoes and bits around the bird. Roast for another 50–60 minutes, or until the chicken juices run clear and the potatoes are crispy and golden.

Remove the chicken to a board and the potatoes to a bowl. Drain some of the chicken fat from the pan (leaving behind the brown chicken juices). Add the butter and spinach to the juices in the hot pan and squeeze in the garlic from the roasted cloves. Stir to coat the spinach. Return to the oven for a few minutes to wilt.

Use a slotted spoon or fish slice to divide the spinach between four plates or shallow bowls. Top with the potatoes, olives and lemons. Carve the chicken (two legs and the top section of each breast, to save plenty for the Ramen, overleaf) and top each portion with some meat. Finally, spoon over the pan juices.

Serves 4, with
leftovers
for ramen
–
Prep 10 mins
–
Cook 1 hour,
30 mins

CHICKEN RAMEN

This is a great contrast to a roast chicken dinner – with plenty of umami flavour and the comfort of a slurp of noodles. Not just for chicken, it's also my favourite thing to do with leftover roast turkey at Christmas. As a bonus, it's super speedy to whip up a batch of this, then customize your finished bowl to taste. The chicken and broth freeze well, so the only dinner prep is boiling your noodles and eggs.

2 tbsp sesame oil, plus extra to serve

240g (9oz) shiitake mushrooms, halved if large

4 spring onions (scallions), greens and whites finely sliced and kept separate

4 garlic cloves, sliced

30g (1oz) fresh ginger, peeled and finely chopped

1.2 litres (5 cups) chicken stock

4 tbsp brown miso paste

1 tbsp dark soy sauce

leftover cooked chicken or turkey, shredded (see page 16)

½ tsp chilli flakes

4 soft-boiled eggs, halved

4 nests of ramen noodles

toasted white or black sesame seeds

chilli or sesame oil (optional)

Add the sesame oil to a large pan over a medium heat. Add the mushrooms, white spring onions and half of the green spring onions and fry for 3 minutes, until the mushrooms are softened. Add the garlic and ginger and fry for 30 seconds before adding the stock along with the miso and soy sauce. Mix together, simmer for 8 minutes and then stir through the chicken and chilli flakes and cook for a final 2 minutes.

Meanwhile, bring a small pan of water to the boil. Add the eggs and boil for 6 minutes before removing from the pan and placing in a bowl of iced water. Peel when cooled and slice in half.

Prepare the noodles according to the packet instructions, then divide between four deep bowls.

Divide the chicken, mushrooms and broth between the bowls and top with two egg halves per portion. Scatter with the remaining green spring onions and sesame seeds, and drizzle with chilli or sesame oil, if liked.

Serves 4
–
Prep 5 mins
–
Cook 15 mins

ROASTED SQUASH WITH TAHINI AND HERBS

Middle Eastern-influenced food is my go-to, especially when it comes to delicious salads. Cooking a whole squash and making two different meals with it is a great way to double up and economize on cooking time. I've used coriander (cilantro), parsley and dill in my grain salad, but any combination is welcome. Spelt is easily swapped for quinoa, cooked rice or lentils.

1 medium–large butternut squash, (approx. 1kg/2lb 2oz) halved, deseeded and sliced into 1.5cm (½in) pieces
2 red onions, each sliced into 10 wedges
4 tbsp olive oil
2 x 250g (9oz) pouches of spelt grains
juice of 1 lemon
15g (½oz) coriander (cilantro), leaves and stalks roughly chopped
10g (¼oz) parsley, leaves and stalks roughly chopped
1 tsp dill, thick stalks discarded and the rest roughly chopped
1 tsp za'atar
salt and freshly ground black pepper

For the tahini dressing
100g (3½oz) tahini
juice of 1 lemon
1 garlic clove, crushed
2 tbsp olive oil
5–6 tbsp water

Preheat the oven to 200°C/180°C fan/400°F/Gas 6. Spread the squash out on one very large baking tray (or two medium-sized ones). Scatter the onions over one half of the squash (or over one of the medium trays) – you want some plain squash left over for the Quiche, overleaf. Season with salt and pepper, then drizzle with 2 tablespoons of olive oil. Roast for 30–40 minutes. Remove from the oven and set aside about 300g (10½oz) of the plain squash for quiche.

Meanwhile, make the tahini dressing. Combine the tahini, lemon juice, garlic and olive oil with 3 tablespoons of water. Use a balloon whisk to combine (it will thicken the more you whisk). Season with salt and pepper, then add another 2–3 tablespoons of water to loosen – you want the texture of natural yoghurt.

Prepare the grains as per the packet instructions. Add the lemon juice and remaining 2 tablespoons of olive oil. Season and mix briefly to combine. Add most of the herbs and mix everything together. Spoon the grains on to a platter then top with the squash and red onions. Drizzle with half the dressing and sprinkle with the za'atar and reserved herbs. Serve with the remaining dressing on the side.

Serves 4,
with leftovers
for quiche
–
Prep 10 mins
–
Cook 40 mins

SQUASH AND GOATS' CHEESE QUICHE

I think my pastry recipe is pretty foolproof, but you can use shop-bought if you want to cut a corner (a 500g/1lb 2oz block of shortcrust will line your tin and leave a little left over). By using pre-roasted squash (see page 20), you save some of the time associated with quiche-making. Goats' cheese and thyme are a great pairing for a delicious lunch or dinner dish that lasts for a few days.

For the pastry

100g (3½oz) salted butter, chilled and cut into rough 1cm (½in) cubes
200g (7oz) plain (all-purpose) flour
3–4 tbsp ice-cold water

For the filling

300g (10½oz) leftover roasted squash (see page 20)
150g (5½oz) goats' cheese (with rind), cut into rough chunks
2 sprigs of thyme, leaves picked
3 eggs, beaten
140ml (scant ⅔ cup) double (heavy) cream
50g (2oz) parmesan, finely grated
salt and freshly ground black pepper

Make the pastry by hand or using a food processor. Rub the butter (or pulse in the food processor) into the flour, until it resembles breadcrumbs. Tip into a bowl (if using the food processor) and add the water, using a butter knife to quickly combine. Pull together into a puck, wrap in cling film (plastic wrap) and chill in the fridge for 30 minutes.

Preheat the oven to 200°C/180°C fan/400°F/Gas 6 and place a baking sheet inside to preheat. Roll the pastry out on a lightly floured surface to circle roughly 26cm (10in) in diameter and 2mm (1/16in) thick. Carefully ease it over the rolling pin then use it to line a 23cm (9in) quiche tin. Pierce the base a few times with the prongs of a fork. Trim any overhang then line with baking parchment and fill with baking beans. Bake for 15 minutes on the preheated baking sheet. Remove the baking beans and parchment and continue to cook for another 5–10 minutes, until lightly golden.

Reduce the oven temperature to 180°C/160°C fan/350°F/Gas 4. Roughly chop the butternut squash and lay on the base of the quiche. Scatter over the goats' cheese and the thyme leaves. Combine the eggs and cream in a bowl with the parmesan. Season, then pour over the quiche filling, being careful not to overflow. Bake on the preheated baking sheet for 25–30 minutes until the top is golden and the egg is set.

Serves 4–6
–
Prep 15 mins, plus chilling
–
Cook 1 hour, 10 mins

One Cook, Two Meals

CHICKEN AND MUSHROOMS

This is a relatively simple but delicious dish that feels special enough to serve to guests (whole chicken legs always feel like quite a statement, I think!). Roasting the chicken on the bone releases all the juices into the mushrooms, making for a super-rich and flavoursome sauce. Plus, there's leftover meat for a Chicken and Mushroom Pie (see overleaf).

450g (1lb) portobello mushrooms, halved then sliced
70g (2½oz) salted butter
2kg (4lb 8oz) chicken legs
2 tbsp olive oil
1 tbsp plain (all-purpose) flour
130ml (generous ½ cup) double (heavy) cream
1 tbsp brandy (optional)
2 sprigs of thyme, leaves picked
2 garlic cloves, crushed
salt and freshly ground black pepper

To serve
10g (¼oz) parsley, chopped
steamed rice or bread
steamed Tenderstem broccoli

Preheat the oven to 200°C/180°C fan/400°F/Gas 6. Add the mushrooms to a large baking tray (or two smaller ones) – I like to use the one that is the same width as the oven. Dot with 50g (2oz) of the butter, then top with the chicken legs. Drizzle the legs with the olive oil and season generously. Bake for 40 minutes.

Remove the mushrooms and juices from the tray, pouring them into a saucepan. Return the chicken to the oven for a final 10 minutes. Add the remaining 20g (¾oz) of butter to a bowl with the plain flour and mix to combine. Whisk into the pan with the mushrooms and juices, followed by the cream, brandy (if using), thyme and garlic. Season with plenty of black pepper. Place over a low heat for a few minutes, stirring until thickened.

Set four chicken legs aside for a pie (see overleaf) and serve the rest with the mushroom sauce poured over, scattered with chopped parsley. Enjoy with boiled rice or hunks of bread, with Tenderstem broccoli on the side.

**Serves 4,
with leftovers
for pie
–
Prep 5 mins
–
Cook 50 mins**

One Cook, Two Meals

CHICKEN AND MUSHROOM PIE

A really decent chicken pie can sometimes be a huge labour of love, but using leftover chicken (already friends with mushrooms) means that this delicious feat only requires 10 minutes of hands-on cooking. It is definitely a wintry comfort, but the light flavours mean it can also be a summery addition alongside sautéed asparagus and courgettes. A slice of this in your lunchbox will definitely sort you out for the afternoon.

3 tbsp olive oil
200g (7oz) chestnut mushrooms, sliced
20g (¾oz) salted butter
2 leeks, washed and finely sliced
2 garlic cloves, crushed
2 tbsp plain (all-purpose) flour
100ml (scant ½ cup) white wine
300ml (1¼ cups) chicken stock
120ml (½ cup) double (heavy) cream
2 tbsp dijon mustard
30g (1oz) tarragon, leaves picked
    and chopped
4 leftover chicken legs (see page 25),
    skin discarded and meat shredded
    into bite-sized pieces
salt and freshly ground black pepper
500g (1lb 2oz) shop-bought puff pastry
1 egg, beaten

To serve (optional)
green veg
mashed potato

Heat the olive oil in a wide frying pan (skillet) over a medium–high heat, then add the mushrooms. Fry for about 5 minutes before reducing the temperature to low and adding the butter and leeks. Cook for another 5 minutes before adding the garlic and cooking for 30 seconds. Stir in the flour, followed by the white wine. Stir it all together before adding the chicken stock, cream, mustard and tarragon. Continue stirring for a few minutes until thickened, then remove from the heat. Stir through the chicken, season, and allow to cool to room temperature.

Preheat the oven to 220°C/200°C fan/425°F/Gas 7. Transfer the filling to a 1.5-litre (52fl oz) shallow pie dish (my filling weighed 1.2kg/2lb 10oz). Roll the pastry out on a lightly floured surface. Brush the rim of the pie dish with egg wash and lay the pastry on top. Use a fork to crimp the pastry on the edge of the pie dish, then trim the excess pastry, leaving a small overhang. Brush the top with more egg wash and make a couple of small slashes in the top with a sharp knife to release steam. Bake for 30 minutes, until risen and golden, and serve with green veg and mashed potato, if liked.

Serves 4–6
–
Prep 5 mins,
plus cooling
–
Cook 40 mins

HEARTY SOUPS

Far heartier — and healthier — than the tinned equivalent, these substantial soups will keep you filled up into the afternoon (especially if teamed with some cheese on toast, as I recommend for the Tomato Soup on page 33). They're the perfect candidate for freezing in a silicone mould and popping out on demand.

THAI-STYLE SPICED BUTTERNUT SQUASH SOUP

I love this soup, combining as it does the heat of a Thai curry with the natural sweetness of butternut squash. It's inspired by something similar I ate on a trek in Chiang Mai, in northern Thailand, and it really warms you through.

4 tbsp sunflower oil
1 medium-large butternut squash
    (approx. 1kg/2lb 2oz), peeled,
    deseeded and chopped into rough
    1.5cm (½in) cubes
2 onions, sliced
4 garlic cloves, crushed
2.5cm (1in) fresh ginger, peeled and
    chopped
150g (5½oz) red curry paste
    (less or more, depending on
    the heat of your paste)
2 x 400ml (14fl oz) tins (cans)
    coconut milk
400ml (1¾ cups) vegetable stock
2 tsp caster (superfine) sugar
1 tbsp fish sauce (optional)
salt and freshly ground black pepper

To garnish
coriander (cilantro) leaves
chilli flakes

Preheat the oven to 200°C/180°C fan/400°F/Gas 6. Add 2 tablespoons of sunflower oil to a large baking tray, followed by the squash cubes. Season, then toss to coat the squash with the oil. Roast for 30 minutes.

Meanwhile, heat the remaining 2 tablespoons of oil in a large saucepan or casserole dish. Add the onions and cook over a medium–low heat for 12–15 minutes, until softened and starting to caramelize. Add the garlic and ginger and fry for another minute before adding the curry paste and frying for a further minute. Add the coconut milk, vegetable stock and sugar, followed by the roasted squash. Bring to the boil then simmer for 10 minutes. Stir through the fish sauce, if using, then blitz using a stick blender until smooth. Serve garnished with coriander leaves and chilli flakes, or portion into containers for freezing (without the garnishes).

Serves 8
–
Prep 10 mins
–
Cook 40 mins

TOMATO SOUP

Wonderfully freezable and utterly comforting, this is the quintessence of a batch cook. Great for a crowd (recommended accompaniment: cheese on toast) or for portioning out for a week of lunches, or freezing for desperate times. All you need is a stockpot!

2 tbsp olive oil
2 onions, chopped
3 celery sticks, chopped
1.6kg (3lb 8oz) tomatoes (mix of cherry
    and regular), chopped into pieces
    the size of half a cherry tomato
3 tbsp tomato purée (paste)
2 tbsp tomato ketchup
1 tsp garlic granules
1 tsp celery salt
1 tbsp caster (superfine) sugar
250ml (generous 1 cup) chicken or
    vegetable stock
220ml (scant 1 cup) double
    (heavy) cream, plus extra to taste
    and to serve
salt and freshly ground black pepper

Heat the olive oil in a stockpot over a medium heat. Add the onion and celery and cook for 6–8 minutes, until softened. Add the tomatoes, followed by the purée, ketchup, garlic granules, celery salt and sugar. Stir for a minute before adding the stock. Bring to the boil, then put a lid on and simmer for 30 minutes. Season before blitzing with a stick blender until smooth (see tip, below). Add the cream and mix to combine (adding more cream to taste, if liked). Spoon into bowls and top with an extra drizzle of cream, or portion into containers for freezing.

Tip
For an extra-smooth soup, blitz in a high-speed blender.

Serves 8–10
–
Prep 10 mins
–
Cook 40 mins

Hearty Soups

MUSHROOM SOUP

This soup is so umami-rich and fully fragrant. I used a combination of shiitake, chestnut (cremini) and portobello mushrooms, but you can use whatever is most easily accessible. The miso gives some extra depth and the stilton has a complementary salty tang.

2 tbsp olive oil
50g (2oz) butter
1kg (2lb 2oz) mixed mushrooms
    (such as shiitake, chestnut/cremini
    and portobello), roughly chopped
4 garlic cloves, crushed
30g (1oz) dried porcini mushrooms,
    soaked in boiling water for
    20 minutes then drained and
    roughly chopped
1.3 litres (generous 5 cups) vegetable
    stock
1 tbsp white miso paste
100ml (scant ½ cup) double
    (heavy) cream, plus extra to garnish
200g (7oz) blue stilton, plus extra
    to garnish
salt and freshly ground black pepper

Set a big stockpot or saucepan over a high heat. Add the oil and butter and then all the mushrooms and fry, stirring every now and then, until all the moisture has evaporated and the mushrooms are well browned. This should take around 18–20 minutes but will depend on the surface area of your pan. Reduce the heat, add the garlic and chopped porcini mushrooms and fry for another minute. Add the stock and miso and simmer for 10 minutes. Remove from the heat and add the cream and 150g (5½oz) of the stilton. Using a stick blender, blitz until smooth and check the seasoning. Spoon into bowls and top with an extra drizzle of cream and a crumble of stilton, or portion into containers for freezing (without the garnishes).

> **Serves 8**
> —
> **Prep 10 mins**
> —
> **Cook 30 mins**

MINESTRONE

This is my favourite soup/stew hybrid for when I want something as simple as soup for lunch or dinner, but need the carb comfort – even better with a hunk of bread slathered in butter. Rich, tomatoey flavour with some kale stirred through, this soup has the perfect balance. Top with parmesan or cheddar for a finishing touch.

4 tbsp olive oil
2 small onions, chopped
2 celery sticks, diced
2 carrots, peeled and diced
2 garlic cloves, crushed
4 tbsp tomato purée (paste)
2 x 400g (14oz) tins (cans) tomatoes
1.5 litres (6 cups) vegetable stock
2 sprigs of thyme, leaves picked
1 tsp caster (superfine) sugar
120g (4¼oz) small dried pasta (I used ditalini rigati)
150g (5½oz) kale, thick stalks removed and leaves roughly chopped
greated parmesan (or cheddar), to serve

Heat the oil in a large pan over a medium heat, then add the onions, celery and carrots. Sauté for 10–12 minutes, until softened, then add the garlic and fry for 30 seconds. Add the tomato purée and cook for 2 minutes, until starting to darken. Add the tomatoes, stock, thyme and sugar. Bring to the boil, then simmer for 20 minutes. Stir through the pasta and kale and continue to cook for another 14–16 minutes, or until the pasta is cooked. Serve with a grating of cheese, or portion into containers for freezing (without the cheese).

> **Serves 8**
> –
> **Prep 10 mins**
> –
> **Cook 50 mins**

CREAMY ONION SOUP

The slicing of this amount of onions might be a mindful task to some, but I prefer to shove mine through a food processor fitted with the slicing blade, which shaves the job down to 5 minutes. This is halfway to being a French onion soup, with the slowly cooked, sweetened onions, but I've made it generally creamier by blitzing half the mixture. The nutty, oozy gruyère topping is obligatory.

2 tbsp olive oil
50g (2oz) butter
1.4kg (3lb 1oz) onions,
    finely sliced
4 garlic cloves, crushed
1 tbsp plain (all-purpose) flour
2 tsp caster (superfine) sugar
50ml (scant ¼ cup) brandy
1.4 litres (scant 6 cups) beef or
    vegetable stock
1 tsp dijon mustard
salt and freshly ground black pepper

To serve
grated gruyère
toast

Add the olive oil and butter to a large casserole dish and place over a medium heat. When the butter has melted, add the onions and cook for 6–7 minutes, until the moisture starts to evaporate. Reduce the heat to low and continue to cook for 35–40 minutes, stirring often. Add the garlic and flour and fry for 30 seconds before adding the sugar and brandy. Increase the heat and cook for a minute, then add the stock and mustard. Boil for 10 minutes. Blitz the soup a little, using a stick blender, so that some is smooth and the rest still has texture. Season to taste.

Spoon into bowls and top with some gruyère (if you're using heatproof bowls you can pop them under the grill, if you like) and serve with toast, or portion into containers for freezing (without the cheese).

Serves 8
–
Prep 15 mins
–
Cook 1 hour

Hearty Soups

RED PEPPER, ALMOND AND PECORINO SOUP

Sweet and tangy with the char of the red (bell) peppers, the sharpness of the vinegar and the delicious creaminess of the cheese, this soup is a hearty winter meal. Pair with some bubbly focaccia to make it even more wholesome.

5 tbsp olive oil, plus extra to serve
3 red (bell) peppers, deseeded and sliced
2 red onions, thinly sliced
6 garlic cloves, 4 crushed and 2 left whole
2 tsp sweet smoked paprika
1.2 litres (5 cups) vegetable or chicken stock
200g (7oz) lightly toasted flaked almonds
450g (1lb) jar roasted red (bell) peppers, drained (350g/12oz drained weight)
70ml (¼ cup) sherry vinegar
75g (2½oz) grated pecorino
10g (¼oz) parsley, chopped, to serve

Heat 2 tablespoons of the oil in a big casserole dish or stockpot over a medium heat. Add the peppers and onions and cook for 20 minutes, until softened and caramelizing. Add the crushed garlic and paprika and fry for another minute before adding the stock, almonds and roasted red peppers. Bring to the boil and then simmer for 10 minutes. Remove from the heat and add the sherry vinegar, the remaining two garlic cloves and 3 tablespoons of olive oil, along with the pecorino. Blitz until smooth (I recommend using a high-speed blender because of the nuts). Serve topped with a drizzle of oil and a sprinkling of parsley, or portion into containers for freezing (without the garnishes).

Serves 8
—
Prep 10 mins
—
Cook 30 mins

CHICKPEA AND LENTIL SOUP

This north African-inspired dish is partway between soup and stew. Thick, tangy and deliciously spiced, it is packed full of protein with the hearty chickpeas and lentils stirred through. The Moroccan equivalent is often made with meat, but I love the flavours in my vegetarian version.

1 tbsp sunflower oil
1 onion, chopped
2 celery sticks, finely chopped
20g (¾oz) fresh ginger, peeled and
    chopped into small matchsticks
1 tsp ground turmeric
2 tsp ground coriander
1 tsp ground cinnamon
2 tbsp rose harissa paste
2 vine tomatoes, roughly chopped
2 tbsp tomato purée (paste)
2 x 400g (14oz) tins (cans)
    chopped tomatoes
400ml (1¾ cups) vegetable
    or chicken stock
2 x 400g (14oz) tins (cans) green
    lentils, drained
1 x 570g (1lb 4oz) jar queen
    chickpeas, drained
100g (3½oz) baby spinach
15g (½oz) coriander (cilantro), chopped
zest and juice of 1 lemon, plus wedges,
    to serve

Put a large saucepan or stockpot over a medium heat. Add the sunflower oil and fry the onion and celery for 5–7 minutes until softened and fragrant. Add the ginger and fry for another minute before adding the spices and harissa paste with the chopped vine tomatoes and tomato purée. Continue to cook for another 2 minutes before adding the chopped tomatoes and stock. Simmer for 15 minutes. Stir though the lentils and chickpeas and cook for 4 minutes before stirring in the spinach until wilted. Remove from the heat and add the coriander, lemon zest and lemon juice. Serve with extra lemon wedges, if liked, or portion into containers for freezing (without the coriander).

Serves 8
–
Prep 10 mins
–
Cook 30 mins

BEETROOT SOUP

Sweet, earthy and the right amount of rich, this soup is a great one to have in your repertoire (just remember to check your teeth afterwards!). Considering beetroot can be quite divisive, the flavours here all combine to make a really well-rounded bowl of hearty soup, topped off with a dollop of crème fraîche. Delicious hot or cold.

2 tbsp olive oil
2 red onions, finely chopped
4 garlic cloves, crushed
2 tsp fennel seeds
2 x 500g (1lb 2oz) bunches of beetroot (beets), leaves and roots discarded, beetroot peeled and chopped into roughly 1.5cm (½in) cubes
1.6 litres (6 cups) vegetable stock
1 tbsp red wine vinegar
salt and freshly ground black pepper

To serve
8 tbsp crème fraîche
10g (¼oz) dill, leaves picked
croutons (homemade or shop-bought)

Heat the olive oil in a large saucepan. Add the onions and sauté for 7 minutes, until soft. Add the garlic and fennel seeds and fry for 30 seconds before adding the beetroot. Add the stock and bring to the boil before reducing to a rapid simmer and cooking for 15–20 minutes, until the beetroot is soft. Add the vinegar and season.

Blitz the soup using a stick blender or food processor. Spoon into bowls and serve topped with a generous dollop of crème fraîche, a scattering of dill fronds, croutons and a good grind of black pepper, or portion into containers for freezing (without the garnishes).

Serves 8
–
Prep 10 mins
–
Cook 30 mins

TRAYBAKES

These recipes minimize fuss with a one-tray finale. The Moussaka and Fish Pie (see pages 56 and 48) are slightly more involved, but the result is a bubbling and delectable meal — sufficient to present to a large group, or to set you up for a week of pre-prepped lunches or dinners. Try roasting up a massive tray of Mediterranean vegetables (see page 50) to jazz up all sorts of lunchboxes.

FISH PIE

This is a massively comforting and nostalgic dish. My memories of fish pie feature a filling that was often a bit wet, laced with discoloured egg slices. None of that here! Putting a bit of cheese in the white sauce gives it a richness that is very welcome, and using smoked fish injects a lot of flavour. It's a hit with adults and kids alike.

For the topping

2kg (4lb 8oz) maris piper (or yukon gold) potatoes, peeled and chopped into rough 2.5cm (1in) chunks
100g (3½oz) salted butter, plus extra for topping
200ml (generous ¾ cup) whole milk
salt and freshly ground black pepper

For the filling

60g (2⅓oz) salted butter
60g (2⅓oz) plain (all-purpose) flour
600ml (2½ cups) whole milk
200g (7oz) cream cheese
75g (2½oz) cheddar, grated
120g (4¼oz) smoked salmon, roughly chopped
350g (12oz) skinless smoked haddock (or other white fish), chopped into 2cm (¾in) pieces
320g (11oz) skinless cod, chopped into 2cm (¾in) pieces
200g (7oz) uncooked king prawns (jumbo shrimp)
250g (9oz) frozen peas
10g (¼oz) parsley, roughly chopped
salt and freshly ground black pepper

Preheat the oven to 180°C/160°C fan/350°F/Gas 4.

Start with the topping. Bring a large pan of salted water to the boil, then add the potatoes and cook for 15–20 minutes, until soft. Drain thoroughly, then add the butter, milk and some salt and black pepper. Mash until smooth.

Meanwhile, make the fish pie filling. Melt the butter in a large saucepan over a low heat and then add the flour. Mix to a smooth paste and continue to cook for a minute, then start to add the milk a little at a time. Use a balloon whisk to combine, mixing until smooth between additions. Remove from the heat and stir through the cream cheese and cheddar. Season with plenty of cracked black pepper. Carefully stir through the fish, prawns, peas and parsley.

Spoon the fish mixture into a 20 x 25cm (8 x 10in) dish. Top with the mashed potato, making indents with the back of a spoon. Dot with some extra butter. Bake for 30 minutes until bubbling and golden.

Tip

Cook one, save one. If you're cooking for a smaller crowd, divide the fish pie filling and mashed potato topping between two 15 x 20cm (6 x 8in) dishes. Cook one, and allow the second to cool before wrapping thoroughly in cling film (plastic wrap) and freezing. To cook from frozen, cook for 1–1½ hours at 200°C/180°C fan/400°F/Gas 6 until piping hot all the way through. If planning to freeze portions, make sure to only use fresh fish in the making of the dish.

Serves 18
–
Prep 35 mins
–
Bake 50 mins

ROASTED VEGETABLES

This might seem like an overly simple recipe, but it's the key to getting some easy, bright veg into your diet. These can be stirred into a grainy salad and topped with crumbled goats' cheese, piled on top of a sheet of puffed pastry and drizzled with pesto or added to a pasta sauce for some last-minute texture. Make a batch and then freeze to use as and when you need.

3 red onions, cut into wedges
3 courgettes (zucchini), sliced into
    0.5cm (¼in) rounds
3 (bell) peppers, mixed colours, sliced
    into 1cm (½in) strips
450g (1lb) cherry tomatoes, on the vine
4 garlic cloves, skin on
4 tbsp olive oil
4 sprigs of thyme, leaves picked
salt and freshly ground black pepper

Preheat the oven to 220°C/200°C fan/425°F/Gas 7. Put all the vegetables into your biggest baking tray, or two medium ones. Scatter with the garlic cloves, then combine the olive oil and thyme in a small bowl and drizzle over everything. Season, then cook for 40–45 minutes, turning halfway through. Squeeze the roasted garlic cloves from their skins to mix into the oil, and remove the vines from the cherry tomatoes before serving.

Serves 8
–
Prep 10 mins
–
Cook 45 mins

CHICKEN THIGHS WITH DATES AND OLIVES

This is one of those dishes that can transfer easily from being a hearty midweek meal to a delicious feast for weekend entertaining. Whichever way you make it, the leftovers make for a great lunch *al-desko* or something to squirrel away in the freezer to resurface for an emergency dinner. Sweet, salty and rich, it's a perfectly balanced meal.

2kg (4lb 8oz) chicken thighs
  (12–16 thighs)
20g (¾oz) oregano, leaves picked
120g (4¼oz) drained pitted green olives
4 tbsp drained capers
250g (9oz) medjool dates, pitted
  and roughly chopped
4 tbsp red wine vinegar
4 tbsp olive oil
150ml (⅔ cup) white wine
2 tbsp honey
2 tbsp soft light brown sugar
8 garlic cloves, crushed
salt and freshly ground black pepper
couscous or rice, to serve

Preheat the oven to 200°C/180°C fan/400°F/Gas 6.

Lay the chicken thighs on a large, slightly lipped baking tray. Scatter the oregano, olives, capers and dates around the chicken. Season the chicken skin. In a jug, combine the vinegar, oil, white wine, honey, sugar and garlic. Pour the liquid around the chicken and then bake for 45 minutes, shuffling the thighs and olives halfway through, or until the chicken juices run clear and the skin is golden.

Serve over couscous or rice.

Serves 8
—
Prep 10 mins
—
Cook 45 mins

LOADED POTATO SKINS

Baked potatoes are an unrivalled comfort food – and pre-filling the skins is a great way of maxing out the batch cook. Freezing the filled skins means they just need a piping-hot reheat for an easy feed for adult or child!

8 medium jacket (baking) potatoes, scrubbed
2 tbsp sunflower oil
50g (2oz) salted butter
3 tbsp double (heavy) cream
220g (8oz) smoked streaky bacon
200g (7oz) grated cheddar, plus extra for topping
salt and freshly ground black pepper

To serve
soured cream
chopped chives

Preheat the oven to 200°C/180°C fan/400°F/Gas 6. Rub the potatoes with 1 tablespoon of the sunflower oil and then season with salt and black pepper. Place on a baking tray and cook for 1 hour to 1 hour 10 minutes, until crisp on the outside and soft in the middle (test with the tip of a kitchen knife, or a skewer). Leave to cool for 10 minutes before slicing each potato in half and carefully scooping out the flesh into a bowl. Mash in the butter and cream and season well.

While the potato is cooling, prepare the bacon. Place a medium frying pan (skillet) over a medium–high heat and add the remaining 1 tablespoon of sunflower oil. Add the bacon and cook for 1½–2 minutes on each side, until crispy – you might need to do this in two batches. Drain on paper towel, then finely chop. Add to the mashed potato along with the cheddar and mix to fully combine. Carefully spoon the mixture back into the potato skins. At this point you can either chill the potatoes to do the final cook another day, or freeze (see tip, below).

To finish, top with extra cheddar and return the skins to the oven to cook for 15 minutes until golden. Serve with soured cream and chives.

Tip
To cook from frozen, defrost overnight then cook for 20–25 minutes in an oven preheated to 200°C/180°C fan/400°F/Gas 6, until piping hot all the way through.

Serves 8
–
Prep 15 mins
–
Cook 1½ hours

MOUSSAKA

Moussaka, like Lasagne (see page 11) is another slightly labour-intensive dish, so it makes sense to make it in bulk to get the reward of a good few portions for less washing up! My take on this classic Greek dish, with layers of aubergine (eggplant) and rich, spiced lamb, is topped with a béchamel sauce for ultimate comfort-eating.

8 tbsp olive oil
4 aubergines (eggplants), cut into
  1cm (½in) slices
2 onions, chopped
3 garlic cloves, crushed
2 tsp ground cinnamon
2 tsp dried oregano
800g (1lb 12oz) minced (ground) lamb
2 tbsp tomato purée (paste)
1 x 400g (14oz) tin (can)
  chopped tomatoes
150ml (⅔ cup) red wine
50g (2oz) salted butter
50g (2 oz) plain (all-purpose) flour
500ml (2 cups) whole milk
100g (3½oz) parmesan, grated
3 egg yolks

Preheat the oven to 220°C/200°C fan/425°F/Gas 7. Using two large baking trays, spread each with 2 tablespoons of olive oil and then top with a layer of aubergine. Drizzle an extra 2 tablespoons of olive oil over each tray and pop in the oven to bake for 20–25 minutes, turning the slices halfway through. Reduce the temperature to 200°C/180°C fan/400°F/Gas 6 once the aubergine has cooked.

Meanwhile, add the onion, garlic, cinnamon, oregano and lamb to a large pan over a medium–high heat and cook, stirring, for 10 minutes, until the mince is browned and the onions softened. Add the tomato purée, chopped tomatoes and red wine and allow to bubble for 15 minutes, until thickened.

To make the béchamel, melt the butter in a large saucepan over a low heat and then add the flour. Mix to a smooth paste and continue to cook for a minute, then start to add the milk a little at a time. Use a balloon whisk to combine, mixing until smooth between additions. Simmer until thickened – this should take about 4 minutes. Remove from the heat and whisk in the parmesan, then set aside to cool slightly while you assemble the layers.

In a 25 x 35cm (10 x 14in) dish, use a third of your cooked aubergine to make a layer. Top with half of the meat mixture, followed by another third of aubergine. Add the rest of the meat and then top with the last of the aubergine. Whisk the egg yolks into the béchamel and spoon it over the meat. Bake for 30 minutes, until browned on top and bubbling. Serve with a side salad.

Serves 8
–
Prep 15 mins
–
Cook 1¼ hours

MACARONI CHEESE

Triple cheese, plus bacon and a breadcrumb topping – this macaroni cheese ticks all the boxes. The sauce-to-pasta ratio means that it's really cheesy and delicious. It'll set you up for the week as your main meal, or a side with a bit of chicken or breaded fish.

1 tbsp sunflower oil
220g (8oz) smoked streaky bacon
600g (1lb 5oz) dried macaroni or spirali pasta
70g (2½oz) salted butter
70g (2½oz) plain (all-purpose) flour
1 litre (4 cups) whole milk
1 tbsp dijon mustard
300g (10½oz) cheddar
100g (3½oz) parmesan, grated, plus an extra 50g (2oz) for topping
1 ball of mozzarella (125g/4½oz drained weight), drained on paper towel
75g (2½oz) fresh breadcrumbs

Place a medium frying pan (skillet) over a medium–high heat and add 1 tablespoon of sunflower oil. Add the bacon and cook for 1½–2 minutes on each side, until crispy – you might need to do this in two batches. Drain on paper towel, then finely chop. Preheat the oven to 200°C/180°C fan/400°F/Gas 6.

Meanwhile, bring a large pan of salted water to the boil. Add the pasta and cook for a minute less than the packet instructions. Drain and return to the pan (off the heat).

While the pasta is cooking, melt the butter in a large saucepan over a low heat and then add the flour. Mix to a smooth paste and continue to cook for a minute, then start to add the milk a little at a time. Use a balloon whisk to combine, mixing until smooth between additions. When all the milk is added, increase the heat slightly and bubble for 3 minutes until beginning to thicken. Remove from the heat, then stir through the mustard, cheddar and 100g (3½oz) of parmesan until melted.

Add the chopped bacon to the pasta and stir through, then pour in the cheese sauce. Mix to combine, then pour into a 25 x 35cm (10 x 14in) baking tray. Top with the mozzarella, torn into pieces, followed by the breadcrumbs and finally the extra parmesan. Bake for 20 minutes until golden and bubbling.

Tip
Refrigerate or freeze any leftovers, then, to reheat without the macaroni cheese drying out, add 1 tablespoon of milk per portion and cook in a pan on the stove, or in the microwave, until piping hot all the way through.

Serves 8
–
Prep 15 mins
–
Cook 35 mins

TUNA AND SWEETCORN PASTA BAKE

I'm a big fan of tinned sweetcorn, despite my age – and this dish is the perfect hybrid of kids' tea and an adult feast. With only the slightest hint of mustard, it can go under the radar for the young ones, but the grown-ups still get to enjoy the elevation of a magically simple pasta bake. Fit for a crowd or easily reheated, or even eaten cold throughout the week.

600g (1lb 5oz) dried fusilli pasta
70g (2½oz) salted butter
70g (2½oz) plain (all-purpose) flour
1 litre (4 cups) whole milk
250g (9oz) grated cheddar, plus
    an extra 50g (2oz) for topping
1 tbsp dijon mustard
3 x 145g (5oz) tins (cans) tuna in spring
    water, drained
2 x 340g (12oz) tins (cans) sweetcorn
    (corn), drained
50g (2oz) mayonnaise
salt and freshly ground black pepper

Preheat the oven to 180°C/160°C fan/350°F/Gas 4. Bring a large pan of salted water to the boil. Add the pasta and cook for 2 minutes less than the packet instructions.

Meanwhile, add the butter to a large saucepan and place over a low heat. When melted, add the flour and use a balloon whisk to mix together. Add the milk a few tablespoonfuls at a time to start with, whisking to a smooth paste, and slowly loosening with more milk. When all the milk has been incorporated, increase the heat and simmer until thickened (about 4–5 minutes). Add the cheddar and mix to melt, off the heat. Stir through the mustard.

In a bowl, mix the tuna, sweetcorn and mayonnaise and season with salt and black pepper.

When the pasta is cooked, drain and add back into the pan (off the heat). Stir through the tuna sweetcorn mix before pouring in the cheese sauce. Mix it all together, adding more seasoning to taste. If you're eating it in one sitting, spoon into a large baking dish, roughly 30 x 20cm (12 x 8in) (or see tip, below). Top with the remaining grated cheddar and bake for 20 minutes until lightly golden.

Tip

If you're not eating it all at once, refrigerate or freeze in portions and reheat on demand. Either defrost it in the fridge overnight or using the defrost mode on the mirowave, then cover with foil and bake for 20 minutes in an oven preheated to 200°C/180°C fan/400°F/Gas 6. Remove the foil, then bake for another 10 minutes, until golden and piping hot all the way through.

Serves 8
–
Prep 10 mins
–
Cook 30 mins

WINTER WARMERS

Seven wonderful ways to get you through those cold winter months (one for each day of the week?), full of wholesome pulses and some warming spices. A mixture of longer and slower cooks, there's something here for every mood — the common trend being comfort!

SWEET POTATO AND SPINACH DHAL

High in both protein and comfort, a big pan of dhal is super easy to whip up en masse. With a subtle blend of spices and the additional sweetness of the sweet potato, this freezes excellently but also lasts well in the fridge – perhaps needing a little loosening with some extra water. It's a great side for a piece of chicken or in a spread with a few other Indian-inspired dishes.

1 tbsp sunflower oil
1 onion, finely chopped
2 garlic cloves, crushed
1 tbsp hot curry powder
2 tsp ground cinnamon
1 tbsp ground cumin
1 tbsp ground coriander
3 dried or fresh curry leaves
2 green chillies, deseeded and
   finely chopped
400g (14oz) red split lentils,
   rinsed twice in cold water
2 x 400ml (14fl oz) tins (cans)
   coconut milk
800ml (3¼ cups) water
500g (1lb 2oz) sweet potatoes,
   peeled and chopped into rough
   2cm (¾in) cubes
260g (9¼oz) baby spinach
15g (½oz) coriander (cilantro),
   roughly chopped
salt and freshly ground black pepper
steamed rice, to serve

Put a large pan over a medium heat. Add the oil followed by the onion and cook for 4–5 minutes, until softened. Add the garlic, spices, curry leaves and green chillies and fry for another 30 seconds before adding in the lentils, coconut milk, water and the sweet potatoes. Bring to the boil, then simmer for 30 minutes. Stir through the spinach until wilted. Taste and season with salt and black pepper, if required, then serve either on its own or with rice, scattered with the coriander.

Serves 8
–
Prep 10 mins
–
Cook 35 mins

CAPONATA

This is inspired by the Sicilian aubergine (eggplant) stew – fried aubergines coated in a thick agrodolce sauce, with delicious pops of brined capers and olives, plus the sweet kick of raisins. I go a bit heavier with the tomatoes than other traditionalists might because I love a richer sauce. Chilli flakes give a background warmth, but feel free to omit them. It's commonly served at room temperature so is great for prepping ahead.

8 tbsp olive oil, plus extra for drizzling
5 aubergines (eggplants) (approx.
  1.2kg/2lb 10oz), cut into rough
  2cm (¾in) dice
4 large celery sticks, halved
  lengthways then sliced
3 red onions, sliced
4 garlic cloves, crushed
600g (1lb 5oz) vine tomatoes,
  roughly chopped
100ml (scant ½ cup) red wine vinegar
1 tbsp caster (superfine) sugar
1 tsp chilli flakes (optional)
680g (1lb 8oz) jar passata
  (strained tomatoes)
150g (5½oz) green olives,
  pitted and roughly chopped
125g (4½oz) capers
180g (6⅓oz) raisins
salt and freshly ground black pepper

To serve
bread, pasta or steamed rice
30g (1oz) toasted flaked almonds
20g (¾oz) parsley, roughly chopped

Heat 2 tablespoons of the olive oil in a large casserole dish over a medium–high heat. Add a third of the aubergine and fry for 4–5 minutes, until browned on all sides. Remove to a bowl. Repeat with the remaining aubergine, in batches, adding a further 2 tablespoons of olive oil with each batch. Reduce the heat to medium. Add a final 2 tablespoons of olive oil to the pan and then add the celery and onions. Season with salt then fry for 15 minutes, before adding the garlic and frying for an extra minute. Then add the tomatoes and cook for another 5 minutes, until starting to mush down. Add the vinegar, sugar, chilli flakes, passata, olives, capers and raisins and return the aubergine to the pan. Put the lid on and simmer for 20 minutes, then remove the lid and cook for another 5 minutes. Check the seasoning, adding salt and/or pepper if necessary, then allow to cool to room temperature.

Divide between plates or bowls and serve with whichever carb you fancy. Drizzle with a little extra oil and finish with a scattering of almonds and chopped parsley.

Serves 8
–
Prep 10 mins
–
Cook 1 hour

CHICKPEA AND CAULIFLOWER CURRY

When you make a vegetarian curry as tasty as this, you really don't notice any absence of meat. High in protein and fibre, I adore chickpeas – and feel that a jar of chickpeas (versus the slightly smaller tinned ones) is a really worthwhile investment. Topped with a tangy and sweet DIY chutney, this is a wonderfully warming dish.

2 tbsp sunflower oil
2 onions, chopped
2 tbsp ground cumin
2 tbsp ground coriander
2 tsp ground turmeric
5 garlic cloves, crushed
25g (1oz) fresh ginger, peeled and
    finely chopped
1 green chilli, finely chopped
2 x 400g (14oz) tin (can)
    chopped tomatoes
400ml (1¾ cups) water
1 large cauliflower (about 1.3kg/2lb 14oz),
    broken into small florets
1 x 570g (1lb 4oz) jar chickpeas, drained
10g (¼oz) chopped coriander (cilantro),
    plus extra leaves to serve
2 tsp garam masala

For the chutney
12 pitted medjool dates,
    roughly chopped
120ml (½ cup) boiling water
130ml (generous ½ cup) tamarind paste
1 tsp ground ginger
1 tsp chilli powder

To serve
natural yoghurt
steamed rice or paratha

Add the oil to a large saucepan or casserole dish over a low–medium heat. Add the onions and cook for 6–7 minutes, until softened. Add the spices, garlic, ginger and chilli and fry for another 2–3 minutes, until fragrant. And the chopped tomatoes and water, followed by the cauliflower and chickpeas. Bring to a rapid simmer then put a lid on the pan and cook for 15 minutes, until the cauliflower is soft but not falling apart. Stir through the coriander and garam masala.

Meanwhile, add the dates to a measuring jug with the boiling water. Leave for 10 minutes before adding the tamarind paste, ground ginger and chilli powder. Blitz with a stick blender until smooth.

Serve the curry with a dollop of yoghurt and a generous drizzle of the tamarind chutney, plus a final scattering of coriander. Delicious with rice or, my favourite, paratha.

> **Serves 8**
> –
> **Prep 10 mins**
> –
> **Cook 25 mins**

BAKED
BEANS

Everyone needs to have a recipe for homemade baked beans up their sleeve! It's a speedy batch cook and much more wholesome and hearty than just pinging open a can. Whipping up a big pan of it and then freezing as portions means you'll always have a secret stash to load up a baked potato or pile on top of toast.

3 tbsp olive oil
2 onions, finely chopped
2 carrots, finely chopped
3 celery sticks, finely chopped
3 garlic cloves, crushed
2 tsp sweet smoked paprika
3 tbsp tomato purée (paste)
2 x 400g (14oz) tins (cans) chopped
    tomatoes
2 x 570g (1lb 4oz) jars haricot beans,
    drained
2 tbsp white wine vinegar
1 tbsp caster (superfine) sugar
salt and freshly ground black pepper

To serve
baked potatoes, toast or bread
plenty of grated parmesan

Add the oil to a large casserole dish or non-stick saucepan and fry the chopped onion, carrot and celery for 10 minutes. Add the garlic, paprika and tomato purée and cook for 1 minute.

Add the chopped tomatoes, drained beans, vinegar and sugar then season with salt and black pepper. Simmer for 10–15 minutes, until the sauce has thickened and the beans have softened.

Serve piled into a buttery baked potato, onto toast or in a bowl with a hunk of bread – either topped with freshly grated parmesan.

Serves 8
–
Prep 10 mins
–
Cook 25 mins

BUTTER BEANS WITH KALE AND PANCETTA

This rich concoction will take your bean game on to a new level. Salty, very lightly spiced and finished with some zingy lemon zest, this really puts the butter bean in the limelight. I recommend using jars of beans because they tend to be much thinner skinned and... more buttery!

2 tbsp olive oil
300g (10½oz) diced pancetta
2 onions, finely sliced
3 garlic cloves, crushed
1 red chilli, deseeded and
    finely chopped
120ml (scant ½ cup) white wine
    (optional)
2 x 700g (1lb 9oz) jars of butter (lima)
    beans, one drained, the other not
400ml (1¾ cups) chicken or
    vegetable stock
250g (9oz) chopped kale, tough
    stalks removed
140g (5oz) finely grated pecorino,
    plus extra to serve
20g (¾oz) salted butter
zest and juice of 1 lemon
toast, to serve

Add the oil to a large casserole dish or saucepan over a medium heat. Add the pancetta and fry for 6–7 minutes, until golden brown. Remove to a bowl with a slotted spoon, then reduce the heat slightly and add the onions. Cook for 7–8 minutes, until softened and turning golden. Add the garlic and chilli before adding the wine, if using, then increase the heat and cook for 1–2 minutes to reduce. Add both the jars of beans and the liquid from one, along with the stock. Gently mash a rough quarter of the beans. Return the pancetta to the pan, bring to a simmer and cook for 15 minutes. Stir through the kale and cook for another 10 minutes. Turn off the heat and stir through the pecorino, butter, lemon zest and juice.

Serve on toast with an extra grating of pecorino.

Serves 8
–
Prep 5 mins
–
Cook 45 mins

MASSAMAN CURRY

The origins of the massaman curry are hotly contested. Rich with tamarind and the added tang of lemongrass, I absolutely adore this slow-cooked beef curry. Putting this in the oven for a couple of hours ensures super-tender meat, sitting alongside new potatoes and little peanut pops.

2 tbsp sunflower oil
2 onions, thinly sliced
1 red chilli, deseeded and chopped, plus extra, sliced, to serve
1 tsp ground cinnamon
400g (14oz) massaman curry paste (300g/10½oz if the paste is spicy)
1.2kg (2lb 10oz) beef shin (shank), cut into 4cm (1½in) chunks
400ml (14fl oz) coconut milk
50ml (scant ¼ cup) tamarind paste
500ml (2 cups) chicken stock
1 lemongrass stick, bashed
2 tbsp brown sugar
1 tbsp fish sauce
100g (3½oz) salted peanuts, plus extra to serve
500g (1lb 2oz) new potatoes, halved or quartered
juice of 1 lime

To serve
steamed rice
coriander (cilantro) leaves
lime wedges

Preheat the oven to 180°C/160°C fan/350°F/Gas 4. Heat the oil in a large casserole dish over a medium–high heat and then add the onions. Cook for 5 minutes, until starting to soften. Add the chopped chilli, cinnamon and curry paste, followed by the beef, and continue to fry for a few more minutes until the beef is beginning to brown. Add the coconut milk, tamarind paste, stock, lemongrass, brown sugar, fish sauce and peanuts. Bring to the boil, then cover and put in the oven for 1 hour 45 minutes.

Meanwhile, put the potatoes into a pan of boiling water and cook for 10–12 minutes, until tender. Drain thoroughly, then add the potatoes to the pan of curry along with the lime juice and return to the oven to cook for the final 15 minutes with the lid off.

Serve the curry with steamed rice topped with chilli slices, extra peanuts and coriander leaves, with lime wedges on the side.

Serves 8
–
Prep 15 mins
–
Cook 2 hours

CHICKEN KORMA

This is such a subtle curry, with gentle spicing and lots of rich, creamy sweetness. Once you've made your own, you might not even want to go back to the takeaway equivalent! Blitzing the onions, garlic and ginger in a food processor makes for some simple prep and a smoother sauce. Win-win.

2 onions, very roughly chopped
6 garlic cloves, peeled
60g (2⅓oz) fresh ginger, peeled and roughly chopped
2 tsp ground turmeric
1 tbsp garam masala
1 tsp mild curry powder
1 tbsp cumin seeds
2 tsp ground coriander
6 cardamom pods, crushed
2 tbsp sunflower oil
1.2kg (2lb 10oz) boneless, skinless chicken thighs, cut into bite-sized pieces
1 x 400g (14oz) tin (can) chopped tomatoes
300ml (1¼ cups) chicken stock
150g (5½oz) ground almonds
100g (3½oz) sultanas (golden raisins)
100ml (scant ½ cup) double (heavy) cream, plus extra to finish
juice of 1 lemon

To serve
steamed rice
toasted flaked almonds

Put the onion, garlic and ginger into a mini food processor with 2 tablespoons of water and blitz until smooth.

Put a pan over a medium heat. Add the spices and fry for 30 seconds until fragrant, then remove to a bowl. Add the oil to the pan, followed by the onion mixture and the chicken. Fry for 15 minutes before returning the spices to the pan and cooking for a further 2–3 minutes. Add the chopped tomatoes, stock, ground almonds and sultanas and simmer for another 10 minutes before stirring through the cream and lemon juice. Serve with rice, drizzled with a little extra cream and a scattering of toasted flaked almonds.

Serves 8
–
Prep 10 mins
–
Cook 30 mins

MEATY
MAINS

Buying quality meat can be quite the indulgence, but doing a batch cook and planning ahead can make that meat go further. Keeping an eye on portion size means that it's all accounted for and you can have a protein fix ready in the freezer whenever you need.

STICKY SHORT RIBS

This dish is guaranteed to make your home smell absolutely delicious – the aroma of slowly braised beef with flavours inspired by East Asia. The cook is slow, but the meltingly tender beef is worth it. Portioning this up to freeze is a stitch in time and means you'll have amazingly juicy short ribs on demand, ready to pile into bao buns or little gem lettuce cups.

2 tbsp sunflower oil
2.5kg (5lb 8oz) short ribs
50ml (scant ¼ cup) rice wine vinegar
70g (2½oz) soft light brown sugar,
   plus 2 tbsp
100ml (scant ½ cup) hoisin sauce
50ml (scant ¼ cup) soy sauce
50g (2oz) fresh ginger, peeled
   and sliced
6 garlic cloves, crushed
3 tsp Chinese five spice
1 litre (4 cups) chicken stock

For the pickled cucumber
100ml (scant ½ cup) rice wine vinegar
80ml (⅓ cup) water
2 tsp salt
1 tsp sugar
1 cucumber, halved lengthways,
   deseeded and thinly sliced

To serve
rice noodles or sticky rice
coriander (cilantro) and mint leaves
   (optional)
sliced chilli (optional)
crispy onions (optional)

Preheat the oven to 165°C/150°C fan/325°F/Gas 3.

Heat 1 tablespoon of sunflower oil in a large casserole dish over a high heat and fry the short ribs in batches, until browned on both sides (it should take about 5 minutes per rib). Set aside on a plate when browned. When you've done all the ribs, carefully pour the rendered fat from the pan into a bowl and set the pan aside for a minute to cool. Once the fat has cooled, discard it (don't pour it down the sink!).

Add the remaining ingredients (apart from the stock) to another bowl. Return the ribs to the casserole dish and top with all the sauce ingredients, followed by the stock. Add up to 500ml (2 cups) of water, if needed, to cover the bones. Scrunch a large sheet of baking parchment and lay this on top of the ribs (try to make the ribs sit in a single layer, if possible). Put the lid on and place the dish in the oven for 4 hours.

While the beef cooks, make the pickled cucumber. Put the vinegar, water, salt and sugar into a small pan and heat until the sugar and salt have dissolved. Put the cucumber into a shallow bowl and pour the vinegar mixture over the top. Let it sit for 30 minutes.

When the meat has cooked and is falling off the bone, use a slotted spoon to remove the beef to a serving dish, discarding the bones. Shred the meat, discarding any fat. Skim as much fat as possible from the casserole of short-rib juices (see tip, below). Put the casserole over a high heat, add 2 tablespoons of sugar and bubble for 5–10 minutes, until reduced and thickened. Toss the meat back through the sauce. Serve the meat with noodles or rice and the drained pickled cucumber. Scatter with herbs, sliced chilli and crispy onions, if wanted.

Tip
To get rid of as much fat as possible, chill the beef overnight and skim off the solidified fat the next day.

Serves 8
–
Prep 10 mins
–
Cook 4½ hours

SWEET AND SOUR PORK

A staple of the Chinese takeaway, you can't argue with the sweet, vinegary tang of a sweet and sour dish. With pops of pineapple and some crunchy vegetables, I choose to lightly coat my pork with cornflour (cornstarch) rather than go for the full deep-fry. A crowd-pleaser and freezer-friendly, this is a simple and delicious fakeaway.

5 tbsp sunflower oil
800g (1lb 12oz) pork loin steaks,
    fat trimmed and cut into
    finger-width strips
7 tbsp cornflour (cornstarch), seasoned
2 onions, cut into 2cm (¾in) chunks
2 red (bell) peppers, deseeded and cut
    into 2cm (¾in) chunks
2 x 425g (15oz) tins (cans) pineapple,
    fruit roughly chopped and
    juice reserved
45g (1¾oz) soft light brown sugar
3 tbsp tomato purée (paste)
100g (3½oz) tomato ketchup
65ml (scant ¼ cup) malt vinegar
65ml (scant ¼ cup) shaoxing rice wine
3 tbsp soy sauce
steamed rice, to serve
3 spring onions (scallions), sliced,
    to garnish

Heat the oil in a big casserole dish over a high heat. Toss the pork in the cornflour in a shallow bowl, then shake off any excess (reserve in the bowl for later) and fry in batches for about 4 minutes, until turning golden. Remove to a plate with a slotted spoon and reduce the heat. Add the onions and peppers and cook for about 6 minutes, until softening but not coloured.

Mix the pineapple juice in a measuring jug with the sugar, tomato purée, ketchup, vinegar, rice wine and soy sauce. Pour a little into the bowl where the pork was tossed with cornflour and use a fork to mix the residual cornflour to a paste.

When the peppers and onions are softened, add the jug of liquid, plus the cornflour mixture, and mix to combine. Add the pork and any resting juices back to the dish, along with the chopped pineapple and simmer for 6–8 minutes, until the sauce is thickened and the pork is cooked through.

Serve with rice and garnish with spring onions.

Serves 8
–
Prep 10 mins
–
Cook 30 mins

CHICKEN WITH CHORIZO AND TOMATOES

Spiced by the delicious, fragrant chorizo, this chicken dish ticks so many boxes. Creamy, sweet and with richness and acidity from the tomatoes, it's a great one-pot dish that will keep you going throughout the week. Serve with bread or rice, or even try in a baked potato.

270g (9½oz) jar sun-dried tomatoes, 4 tbsp oil set aside and drained tomatoes roughly chopped
3 onions, sliced
3 garlic cloves, crushed
1 tsp sweet smoked paprika
225g (8oz) spicy chorizo, cut into 5mm (¼in) half-moons
1.3kg (2lb 14oz) skinless and boneless chicken thighs, cut into bite-sized pieces
400g (14oz) cherry tomatoes, halved
200ml (generous ¾ cup) chicken stock
150ml (⅔ cup) crème fraîche
15g (½oz) basil, roughly chopped
crusty bread or steamed rice, to serve

Put a large casserole dish or saucepan over a medium heat and add 2 tablespoons of oil from the sun-dried tomatoes, followed by the onions. Cook for 7–8 minutes until softened and starting to turn sticky, then add the garlic and sweet smoked paprika and cook for a minute more. Remove to a plate then increase the heat and add the chorizo with 2 more tablespoons of sun-dried tomato oil. Fry for 5–6 minutes until the chorizo golden and releasing its juices. Set the chorizo and onions aside on a plate.

Add the chicken to the pan and cook for 5 minutes, turning regularly, until browned. Add the cherry tomatoes and cook for a couple of minutes before adding the chicken stock and the chopped sun-dried tomatoes. Return the chorizo and onions to the pan then bring to the boil and reduce to a simmer. Simmer for 10 more minutes, then stir through the crème fraîche and basil. Season, then serve with crusty bread or rice.

Serves 8
–
Prep 10 mins
–
Cook 35 mins

PULLED PORK

Slow-cooking pulled pork is a really economical way of feeding a crowd, or stockpiling supplies. With shoulder joints inevitably being at least 1kg (2lb 2oz), you're always going to end up with quite a few portions – so this is a way to lean into it and organize your food supplies. The sauce is super easy to throw together and then the casserole dish does all the hard work for you. Try serving this piled into brioche buns and topped with coleslaw, in tacos with pickled onion and shredded cabbage – or straight up, with a side of macaroni cheese.

1.5kg (3lb 5oz) pork shoulder joint
4 tsp sweet smoked paprika
2 tsp ground cumin
2 tsp ground coriander
4 garlic cloves, crushed
1 tbsp salt flakes
2 tbsp soft light brown sugar
400ml (1¾ cups) dry cider
200ml (generous ¾ cup) barbecue sauce
2 tbsp dijon mustard

Preheat the oven to 165°C/150°C fan/325°F/Gas 3.

Trim the skin and most of the fat from the pork joint, then cut in half for extra surface area.

Combine the spices, garlic, salt and sugar in a bowl then rub into the meat. Place in a medium-sized casserole dish. Combine the cider, barbecue sauce and mustard in a jug and pour over the meat – it should come about three-quarters of the way up the pork. Put the lid on and pop in the oven for 4 hours, turning the meat partway-through.

Remove the casserole from the oven and put the meat onto a plate or board, then shred. The remaining sauce should be thick and delicious, but place over a medium heat and boil for a little while, if it is too thin. Return the shredded meat to the casserole, then serve with your choice of accompaniments (see introduction).

Serves 8
–
Prep 10 mins
–
Cook 4 hours

Meaty Mains

SAUSAGE AND FENNEL RAGÙ

A rich and tomatoey ragù that doesn't contain beef! My first try at a sausage ragù felt completely revelatory and converted me on how to make a pack of sausages go further. The spiciness of the Cumberland sausage adds to the subtle warmth of this pasta sauce, and the fennel gives great depth. This freezes really well, and also tastes amazing piled onto toast for a different iteration.

4 tbsp olive oil
10 Cumberland sausages (approx. 700g/1lb 9oz)
1 large fennel bulb, core removed and thinly sliced
2 onions, thinly sliced
3 large garlic cloves, crushed
1 tsp chilli flakes
2 tsp fennel seeds
3 tbsp tomato purée (paste)
60ml (scant ¼ cup) brandy or white wine
3 x 400g (14oz) tins (cans) chopped tomatoes
125ml (½ cup) double (heavy) cream
50g (2oz) finely grated parmesan, plus extra to serve
zest of 1 lemon
linguine, to serve

Heat 2 tablespoons of the olive oil in a large casserole dish over a medium–high heat. Allow to heat up, then squeeze the sausage meat into the pan (discarding the skins, if there are any), breaking the meat up into little 1–2cm (½–¾in) nuggets. Fry, turning often, until golden. Remove to a plate with a slotted spoon, then reduce the heat slightly. Add the remaining 2 tablespoons of olive oil, followed by the sliced fennel and onions. Cook for 15–20 minutes, until softened and starting to caramelize. Add the garlic, chilli, fennel seeds and tomato purée and cook for 1–2 minutes, until fragrant. Add the brandy or white wine and increase the heat until the alcohol has nearly evaporated, scraping the bottom of the dish to release all the browned bits. Add the chopped tomatoes and return the sausage meat to the pan. Bring to the boil, then reduce the heat and simmer for 20 minutes.

Meanwhile, cook the linguine in a large saucepan according to the packet instructions. Drain and return the pasta to the pan (off the heat).

When the ragù has finished simmering, stir through the cream, parmesan and lemon zest. Spoon the appropriate portion of ragù through the freshly cooked linguine and top with a little extra parmesan to serve. Refrigerate or freeze any leftovers and serve with freshly cooked linguine on demand.

Serves 8
–
Prep 15 mins
–
Cook 50 mins

Meaty Mains

SPICED MIDDLE-EASTERN-STYLE LAMB SHOULDER

Slow-cooked shoulder is my favourite way to eat lamb. Shredded and coated in sticky, spiced juices, it is a perfect Saturday night dinner – plus you can shove it in the oven and not think about it for a few hours, freeing up your afternoon so you can do whatever else you need. The leftovers make a great packed-lunch filler.

1.8–2kg (4lb–4lb 8oz) lamb shoulder
3 tsp ground cumin
2 tsp ground cinnamon
1 tbsp za'atar
2 tsp ground coriander
4 garlic cloves, crushed
juice of 2 lemons
2 tbsp olive oil
2 red onions, cut into wedges
250ml (generous 1 cup) chicken stock
2 tbsp honey
200g (7oz) pomegranate seeds,
   to serve

For the salad
250g (9oz) cherry tomatoes, halved
1 cucumber, deseeded and roughly
   chopped into bite-sized pieces
15g (½oz) mint, leaves picked and
   roughly chopped
15g (½oz) coriander (cilantro), roughly
   chopped
juice of 1 lemon
2 tbsp olive oil

For the rice
2 tbsp olive oil
2 onions, thinly sliced
4 garlic cloves, crushed
240g (8½oz) basmati rice

Preheat the oven to 165°C/150°C fan/325°F/Gas 3. Score the flesh of the lamb shoulder. Combine the spices, garlic, the juice of two lemons and the olive oil in a bowl. Remove and discard the seeds from the lemons, roughly chop them and combine them with the onion wedges on the base of a large baking tray. Rub the spice paste over the top and bottom of the lamb, then lay it on top of the lemon and onion wedges. Pour the stock around the meat. Cover tightly with foil and cook for 4½ hours.

Towards the end of the lamb cooking time, combine the tomatoes, cucumber and herbs then toss together with the lemon juice and olive oil.

When the lamb has had its cooking time, spoon the juices, lemon pieces and onion into a saucepan. Return the lamb to the oven for a further 30 minutes. Strain any lamb fat you can from the pan of juices then add the honey. Bring to the boil and keep it bubbling for 5–10 minutes, until reduced and glossy. Remove the lamb from the oven and shred the meat (discarding the bone). Coat in the reduced juices.

Meanwhile, to make the rice, put a medium saucepan over a low–medium heat. Add the olive oil, then the onions and cook for 15–20 minutes, until softened and starting to caramelize. Add the garlic and cook for another minute before adding the rice. Coat in the oil then add 500ml (2 cups) of water. Bring to the boil then simmer, adding extra water if needed. Cook as per the packet instructions. You will either need to drain or add water, depending on the brand of rice.

Serve the lamb with the rice and salad, scattered with pomegranate seeds. Save the leftover lamb to pile into wraps with hummus and salad.

> Serves 4,
> with leftovers
> for wraps
> –
> Prep 20 mins
> –
> Cook 5¼ hours

MEATBALLS

Meatballs with spaghetti always remind me of being served bowls of them, piled high, by my Italian–American uncle. They're decadent, delicious and surprisingly easy to whip up yourself (and you can even get the kids involved, if you want). The meatballs freeze really well, so a batch of these can go a long way. Baking the meatballs avoids the drama and spitting oil of frying up batches.

1 x quantity of Basic Tomato Sauce (see page 118)
100g (3½oz) stale bread, made into breadcrumbs
50ml (scant ¼ cup) whole milk
500g (1lb 2oz) minced (ground) pork
500g (1lb 2oz) minced (ground) beef
80g (2¾oz) grated parmesan, plus extra to serve
1 tbsp dried mixed herbs
1 egg, beaten
3 garlic cloves, crushed
3 tbsp olive oil
salt and freshly ground black pepper

To serve
spaghetti or sub rolls
basil leaves

Preheat the oven to 220°C/200°C fan/425°F/Gas 7. If you're making the tomato sauce fresh, do that before starting the next step. Keep warm.

For the meatballs, add the breadcrumbs and milk to a large bowl and mix to combine.

Add all the remaining meatball ingredients except for the olive oil, then season generously with salt and black pepper. Mix thoroughly with your hands, squeezing all the meat together. Weigh the mixture and then divide into 24 equal-sized portions (mine were about 50g/2oz each). Drizzle 1 tablespoon of olive oil on to a large baking tray and then line up the meatballs on it. Drizzle with another 2 tablespoons of olive oil and then cook for 18–20 minutes, until browned, turning halfway through.

Use a slotted spoon to remove the meatballs from the tray and stir through the tomato sauce. Serve on top of freshly cooked spaghetti topped with extra parmesan and scattered with basil leaves, or spoon into sub rolls.

Tip
These meatballs can be frozen cooked or uncooked. Defrost overnight, then bake in an oven preheated to 220°C/200°C fan/425°F/Gas 7 until piping hot all the way through, adjusting the cook time as needed.

Serves 8
–
Prep 15 mins
–
Cook 20 mins

SUMMER STAPLES

Packed with lighter recipes, this goes to show that batch cooking isn't just for cold weather. With a wonderfully green Orzotto (see page 97) and some chilled soups (see pages 98 and 100) that transport you straight to Spain, these recipes will free up time in your summer diary to enjoy the longer evenings and (hopefully) sun-drenched weekends.

PEA AND ASPARAGUS ORZOTTO

This dish is an amalgam of a risotto and a pasta salad – comforting and hearty but delicious eaten hot or cold. Stirred through with the feta and vegetables, it's wonderfully spring-like. Try swapping asparagus for courgette or Tenderstem broccoli when asparagus isn't in season – or even some charred brussels sprouts for a winter edition.

3 tbsp olive oil
2 onions, finely chopped
3 celery sticks, finely chopped
2 garlic cloves, crushed
500g (1lb 2oz) dried orzo
150ml (⅔ cup) white wine
1.3 litres (generous 5 cups) chicken or
    vegetable stock
400g (14oz) asparagus, trimmed and
    cut into 5cm (2in) lengths
250g (9oz) frozen peas
60g (2⅓oz) cream cheese
15g (½oz) basil, leaves chopped,
    plus extra to serve
200g (7oz) feta

Heat the oil in a casserole dish or large saucepan over a low–medium heat. Add the onions and celery and cook for about 7 minutes, until softened. Add the garlic and cook for another 30 seconds before adding the orzo. Fry for a couple of minutes before adding the wine and increasing the heat. Cook until the wine has evaporated, then add enough stock to cover the orzo. Keep over a low–medium heat and bubble until the stock has started to absorb. Keep topping up and stirring – this should take about 15–20 minutes.

Meanwhile, cook the asparagus in a pan of boiling water for 3 minutes, then drain. Defrost the peas in a bowl of boiling water and then drain.

Off the heat, stir the cream cheese into the orzotto, then fold in the vegetables and basil and crumble in most of the feta. Spoon into bowls and top with the remaining feta and some extra basil.

Tip

If refrigerating your leftovers, you could simply enjoy them cold! Or, to reheat, defrost in the fridge overnight, if frozen. Add to a saucepan and cook over a low–medium heat with a splash of boiling water, until piping hot all the way through.

Serves 8
–
Prep 5 mins
–
Cook 30 mins

Summer Staples

WHITE GAZPACHO

This chilled white soup is the perfect refreshment on a hot day. Inspired by the Spanish version, ajo blanco, it combines almonds and stale bread with cucumbers and grapes to form a well-balanced and surprisingly filling soup.

180g (6⅓oz) lightly toasted flaked almonds, plus a little extra to serve
2 cucumbers, peeled and roughly chopped
600g (1lb 5oz) seedless green grapes, roughly chopped, plus a few extra, sliced, to serve
3 garlic cloves, crushed
200g (7oz) stale white bread, crusts removed and roughly chopped
2 tsp sherry vinegar or white wine vinegar
3 tbsp olive oil, plus extra for drizzling
200g (7oz) Greek yoghurt
1 tsp honey (optional)
salt and freshly ground black pepper
mint leaves, to serve

Soak the almonds for 10 minutes in boiling water, then drain thoroughly. Meanwhile, put the cucumbers and grapes into a food processor and blitz together with a large pinch of salt. Add the almonds with the garlic and the sourdough and blitz together. Finally add the vinegar, olive oil and Greek yoghurt and mix to thoroughly combine. You might then want to transfer to a high-speed blender for a smoother consistency. Check the flavour and season to taste with salt and black pepper, adding more vinegar for a bit more sharpness, or a teaspoon of honey if your grapes aren't too sweet.

Refrigerate for 2 hours then spoon into bowls or divide between storage containers. To serve, drizzle with a little extra olive oil and top with sliced grapes and flaked almonds, plus some mint leaves.

Serves 8
–
Prep 15 mins, plus chilling

SALMOREJO

This soup originates in Andalucía, where inevitably the tomatoes are deliciously ripe and fragrant. This doesn't taste quite as good as it does on holiday, but it's a nod to the thick, chilled soup reminiscent of tapas restaurants and trips to Spain.

240g/8½oz (about 4 slices) stale white bread, crusts removed and roughly chopped
1kg (2lb 2oz) ripe tomatoes, roughly chopped
3–4 garlic cloves, crushed, to taste
150ml (⅔ cup) olive oil, plus extra for drizzling
1 tsp sugar
3–4 tbsp sherry vinegar

To serve (optional)
chopped hard-boiled eggs
anchovies
strips of serrano ham

Put the bread, tomatoes, garlic, olive oil, sugar, 3 tablespoons of sherry vinegar and 100ml (scant ½ cup) of water into a high-speed blender (if large enough) or food processor. Blitz, then taste and add the extra vinegar, if liked. Add extra water until you reach your desired consistency, remembering that salmorejo is traditionally quite thick. Blend until fully combined. If using a food processor, you might then want to transfer the mixture to a high-speed blender, in batches, to ensure a super-silky finish.

Refrigerate for 2 hours before drizzling with a bit of extra oil and adding your choice of toppings.

Serves 8
—
Prep 10 mins, plus chilling

KEDGEREE

Growing up, this dish was probably on a fortnightly rotation. Arriving home from school to the smell of poaching haddock... it's actually not 100 per cent the stuff of fond memories! But the finished dish is lightly spiced and provides maximum comfort. A big vat of it would feed the family and provide leftovers for lunches. Boil your eggs as you go so that they stay super fresh-tasting.

480g (1lb 1oz) smoked haddock (or other smoked white fish)
60g (2⅓oz) salted butter
2 onions, finely chopped
1 tbsp medium curry powder
1 tsp ground cumin
1 tsp ground coriander
1 tsp ground cinnamon
450g (1lb) basmati rice
180g (6⅓oz) frozen peas, defrosted in warm water
180g (6⅓oz) raw, peeled king prawns (jumbo shrimp), defrosted if frozen (see tip)
8 eggs
juice of 1 lemon, plus extra wedges to serve
10g (¼oz) parsley, roughly chopped
salt and freshly ground black pepper
mango chutney or mango amba sauce, to serve (optional)

To poach the fish, set a large casserole dish over a low–medium heat and add 600ml (2½ cups) of water. When simmering, add the haddock and cook for 4–5 minutes. Drain, reserving the liquid in a jug and putting the fish to one side.

Return the casserole to the heat and add the butter, followed by the onions. Cook for 7–8 minutes, until softened, then add the curry powder and spices and fry for another minute. Add the reserved poaching liquid, plus an extra 600ml (2½ cups) of water, followed by the rice. Bring to a simmer and then cook for 10 minutes, adding more water if it starts to look dry. Season with salt and black pepper, then stir through the peas and prawns and put the lid on the casserole. Turn off the heat and let it sit for 5 minutes, or until the prawns have gone pink and are hot through.

Meanwhile, boil the eggs (as many as per portions you are serving immediately). Lower them into a pan of boiling water and boil for 6 minutes for a soft finish or 8 minutes for a hard boil. Drain and add to a bowl of iced water.

Flake the fish into big chunks and discard the skin. Stir the flaked fish, lemon juice and most of the parsley into the kedgeree. Peel and then halve or quarter the eggs.

To serve, spoon the kedgeree into dishes and top with a boiled egg per person. Scatter with the remaining parsley, and finish with a wedge of lemon and a spoonful of mango chutney or mango amba sauce, if liked.

Tip

For food safety reasons, do not re-freeze seafood that has been frozen and defrosted. Only portion this up for freezing and reheating if you have used fresh fish and prawns.

Serves 8
–
Prep 10 mins
–
Cook 30 mins

COURGETTE AND FETA SOUP WITH FRESH PESTO

Courgette (zucchini) isn't something you'd necessarily associate with soup – but this recipe is here to challenge your preconceptions! The subtlety of the slow-cooked courgettes is complemented by a lemony tang and a herby kick from some homemade pesto. And feta is guaranteed to make any dish extra delicious. A leisurely cook, but mostly hands-off, this is a great soup to add to your summer recipe collection.

4 tbsp olive oil
60g (2⅓oz) salted butter
2kg (4lb 8oz) courgettes (zucchini), trimmed and cut into 1cm (½in) discs
5 garlic cloves, crushed
juice of ½ lemon (reserve the other half for the pesto, below)
800ml (3¼ cups) vegetable stock
250g (9oz) feta, crumbled
salt and freshly ground black pepper

For the pesto
30g (1oz) pistachios
30g (1oz) basil, leaves and stalks, plus extra to serve
25g (1oz) parmesan, grated
5 tbsp olive oil
1 garlic clove, crushed
juice of ½ lemon
salt and freshly ground black pepper

Put a big casserole dish over a medium heat and add the olive oil and butter. Add the courgettes, season with salt and black pepper and cook for 10 minutes, uncovered. Add the garlic, stir, then cover and cook for 40 minutes, stirring part-way through. Add the juice of half a lemon and the vegetable stock and remove the lid to cook for a final 10 minutes.

Meanwhile, make the pesto. Toast the pistachios in a small frying pan (skillet) until starting to smell fragrant, then set aside to cool. Add to a pestle and mortar, or the small bowl of a food processor, along with the basil leaves, parmesan, olive oil, crushed garlic and the juice of the remaining half lemon. Season with salt and black pepper and then crush or blitz until combined, adding 2 tablespoons of water to loosen, if needed.

Add half of the feta to the pan of courgettes and blitz half the mixture, using a stick blender – this means you get a nice combination of textures. Stir through 1 tablespoon of pesto. Ladle into bowls and top with the remaining pesto, some crumbled feta and the extra basil leaves, or portion into containers for freezing (without the garnishes).

Serves 8
–
Prep 15 mins
–
Cook 1 hour

LEEK AND CAMEMBERT RISOTTO

Slow-cooked leeks and delicious, creamy camembert make an awesome team, but this is also a really simple staple risotto recipe. This recipe will freeze but the texture changes a little when reheated. It is best enjoyed with a crowd on its first outing, then portioned out through the week.

1.4 litres (6 cups) chicken or
  vegetable stock
100g (3½oz) butter
4 tbsp olive oil
1 onion, finely chopped
2 celery sticks, finely chopped
500g (1lb 2oz) leeks, finely sliced
500g (1lb 2oz) arborio rice
300ml (1¼ cups) white wine
40g (1½oz) parmesan, grated
250g (9oz) camembert, cut into
  rough 1.5cm (½in) chunks
sea salt and freshly ground
  black pepper

Put the stock in a saucepan and place over a low heat. Add 50g (2oz) of the butter and the olive oil to a large casserole dish and place over a low–medium heat. When the butter has melted, add the onion, celery and leeks. Cook for about 15 minutes, stirring, until softened. Increase the heat slightly and add the rice, coating it in the butter and oil, and cook for about a minute. Then add the wine and bubble for a couple of minutes until almost evaporated. Reduce the temperature and start adding the hot stock, a ladleful at a time, letting it absorb between each addition. Continue until the stock has been used up – this will take about 16 minutes but may depend on your rice. Stir through the parmesan and remaining butter, then fold through the camembert. Season with salt and pepper before spooning into bowls to serve.

Tip

To reheat, defrost in the fridge overnight or using the defrost setting on the microwave, if frozen. Then either blast in the microwave or heat in a pan over a low heat with a splash of boiling water until piping hot all the way through.

Serves 8
–
Prep 10 mins
–
Cook 35 mins

FREEZER FILLERS

This is the chapter to open up on a rainy weekend, when you have the energy for some super-efficiency. It could also be called the 'nesting' chapter – for lining your freezer drawers with wholesome gifts for the future! Having a stash of scones (see page 128) ready for an impromptu afternoon treat is such a win.

CHEESE AND HAM CROQUETTES

I think my love for Spain somehow coincided with my discovery of croquettes. I'd only ever known about the potato croquettes the dinner lady lumped on your tray at primary school – and then the world of molten béchamel was opened up to me! These take a few stages of prep, but if you're making one, you might as well make thirty, and these are a joy to discover in the freezer.

80g (2¾oz) salted butter
110g (3¾oz) plain (all-purpose) flour
650ml (generous 2½ cups) whole milk
75g (2½oz) manchego, finely grated
150g (5½oz) cheddar, grated
150g (5½oz) serrano or ibérico ham, finely chopped
75g (2½oz) plain (all-purpose) flour, seasoned with salt and pepper
2 eggs, beaten
150g (5½oz) fine dried breadcrumbs, seasoned with salt and pepper
salt and freshly ground black pepper
sunflower oil, for deep-frying

Melt the butter in a saucepan over a low heat. Add the flour and use a balloon whisk to make a paste. Slowly add the milk, beating well between additions, so you end up with a smooth but thick sauce. Remove from the heat and whisk in the cheeses, then stir through the ham, seasoning generously with salt and pepper.

Transfer to a shallow tray or plastic tub and cool to room temperature, then cover with a lid or cling film (plastic wrap) and refrigerate for 2 hours, or longer.

Prepare your breadcrumbing station by putting the seasoned flour, eggs and half the breadcrumbs into three separate shallow bowls. Line a plate or board with parchment paper. Use a tablespoon to take scoops of the cheesy béchamel mixture. Roll each scoop into a ball using both hands and then roll through the flour, shaking off any excess. I like to start by doing about ten of these and sitting them on a board. Next, roll the balls in the beaten egg – again shaking off any excess – then roll through the breadcrumbs. Place the finished balls on the lined plate or board. Repeat until the mixture is used up, replenishing the breadcrumbs when needed (this stops them getting too eggy). Place the board or plate in the freezer and open-freeze until solid enough to safely transfer to a sealed container or freezer bag.

To cook from frozen, fill a medium pan to approximately 5cm (2in) deep with sunflower oil. Heat the oil to 180°C (350°F). Carefully lower in the croquettes with a slotted spoon and cook in batches for 3½–4 minutes, until golden and piping hot all the way through.

Tip

To eat straight away, chill the crumbed croquettes for 30 minutes (skip the freezing step). Heat the oil as above, then fry for 1½–2 minutes, or until golden and piping hot all the way through.

Makes 30
–
Prep 40 mins, plus chilling
–
Cook 25 mins

SALMON FISHCAKES

I've always loved a fishcake as an easy, oven-ready supper. With a good ratio of potato to flaky fish, they're a self-contained meal. You could swap out the salmon for cod or even tinned tuna, and this is a great way to repurpose leftover mashed potato.

600g (1lb 5oz) salmon fillets
600g (1lb 5oz) maris piper (or yukon gold) potatoes, peeled and cut into roughly 1.5cm (½in) cubes
15g (½oz) butter
zest of 1 lemon
1 tbsp dijon mustard
1 tsp finely chopped dill
1 tsp finely chopped parsley
75g (2½oz) plain (all-purpose) flour
1 large egg, beaten
75g (2½oz) fine dried breadcrumbs
sunflower oil, for brushing
salt and freshly ground black pepper

To serve
tartare sauce
lemon wedges
peas

Preheat the oven to 200°C/180°C fan/400°F/Gas 6. Put the salmon on a baking tray and cook for 10–12 minutes, until opaque and flaking.

Meanwhile, add the potatoes to a saucepan of boiling water and cook for 10 minutes, until tender. Drain, then steam dry by leaving the steaming potatoes in the colander and placing over the empty saucepan, off the heat. Return the potatoes to the pan (off the heat) and add the butter, lemon zest and mustard. Mash until smooth, then flake in the salmon (discarding the skin) and add the dill, parsley and some salt and pepper. Gently fold everything together, so you don't mash the fish too much. Form into eight fishcakes.

Put the flour, egg and breadcrumbs into three separate shallow bowls. Line a plate or board with parchment paper. Dip the fishcakes into the flour to completely cover, shaking off any excess. Dip into the egg, again shaking off any excess, then dip into the breadcrumbs, making sure to fully coat. Place on the lined plate or board and continue with the rest of the fishcakes. Open-freeze until firm, then transfer to a freezer bag or a sealed container.

When ready to eat, preheat the oven to 200°C/180°C fan/ 400°F/Gas 6. Transfer the fishcakes to a baking tray, brush with sunflower oil then put in the oven and cook for 35–40 minutes, until golden and hot through. Serve with tartare sauce, lemon wedges and peas.

Tip
To eat straight away, chill for 30 minutes to firm up before transferring to a baking tray, brushing with oil and cooking in an oven preheated to 200°C/180°C fan/400°F/Gas 6 for 25–30 minutes, until piping hot all the way through.

Serves 8
–
Prep 10 mins, plus chilling
–
Cook 1 hour

GARLIC BREAD

Five minutes of prep for a little freezer store of amazingly crispy, indulgently buttery, wonderfully garlicky baguette. Far better than shop-bought, you can adjust the recipe to your taste – grated mozzarella between the slices also goes down a treat. This goes great with the Bolognaise on page 13 or the Meatballs and spaghetti on page 92.

200g (7oz) salted butter, softened
6 garlic cloves, crushed
1 tsp finely chopped parsley
2 bake-at-home white baguettes
  (300g/10½oz)
salt and freshly ground black pepper

Mash together the butter, garlic and parsley and season. Make eight diagonal incisions into each baguette, making sure you don't cut the whole way through the bread. Spread the butter into each cut, distributing it evenly, then spread any remaining butter over the top of the baguettes. Wrap in cling film (plastic wrap) and freeze.

Preheat the oven to 200°C/180°C fan/400°F/Gas 6. Wrap each baguette in foil then bake for 20 minutes. Peel off the foil and cook for another 10 minutes, until golden.

Serves 8
–
Prep 5 mins
–
Cook 30 mins

SAUSAGE ROLLS

A batch of these in the freezer really is a godsend for so many different occasions – a panicked kids' tea with some baked beans and chips, fuel for a walk, a packed lunch, a snack to tide you over to supper... You could make these rolls half as big if you want them a little more snack-sized, and sub the onion chutney for whatever you have in the fridge.

400g (14oz) sausage meat, or sausages squeezed from their skins (I like to use good-quality Cumberland sausages for a bit of black pepperiness)
1 tbsp dijon mustard
400g (14oz) block shop-bought puff pastry
plain (all-purpose) flour, for dusting
5 tbsp caramelized onion chutney
1 egg, beaten
salt and freshly ground black pepper

Combine the sausage meat, mustard and some salt and pepper in a bowl with 2 tablespoons of water.

Roll the pastry out on a lightly floured surface to 30 x 32cm (12 x 13in). With the short end nearest to you, slice the rectangle in half vertically to make two 15 x 32cm (6 x 13in) strips. Spoon the onion chutney onto the pastry, leaving a 2cm (¾in) border. Divide the sausage meat into two and form into long sausages down the middle of each pastry strip. Brush one length of each pastry strip with some of the beaten egg, fold the pastry over the filling and then use a fork to seal the seams well. Glaze the top with the rest of the egg. Cut each length into four and then put onto a parchment-lined baking tray or plate and open-freeze. When firm they can be transferred to a plastic bag and frozen for up to a month.

To bake, preheat the oven to 200°C/180°C fan/400°F/Gas 6. Transfer the rolls to a baking tray and cook for 35–40 minutes until puffed and golden and piping hot all the way through.

Tip

To eat straight away, chill for 15 minutes, then transfer to a baking tray and place in an oven preheated to 200°C/180°C fan/400°F/Gas 6 for 30–35 minutes, until puffed and golden and piping hot all the way through.

Serves 8
–
Prep 15 mins, plus chilling
–
Cook 40 mins

BASIC TOMATO SAUCE

This is a pretty simple but delicious staple to have up your sleeve/in your freezer. It can be the basis of an arrabbiata (just add chilli!), puttanesca (olives, capers and anchovies) or just straight-up stirred through spaghetti and showered with parmesan. Try it with my Meatball recipe on page 92.

3 tbsp olive oil
4 garlic cloves, crushed
2 x 400g (14oz) tins (cans) chopped
    tomatoes
2 x 500g (1lb 2oz) cartons passata
    (strained tomatoes)
2 tbsp tomato purée (paste)
½ tbsp dried mixed herbs
1½ tbsp sugar
1 tbsp white or red wine vinegar
20g (1oz) salted butter (omit if making
    the sauce vegan)
salt and freshly ground black pepper

Add the olive oil to a large saucepan over a medium–low heat. When hot, add the garlic and fry for 15–30 seconds, until turning fragrant. Add the chopped tomatoes, passata, tomato purée, herbs, sugar and vinegar and season with salt and pepper. Bring to the boil then reduce the heat slightly and simmer rapidly for 15–20 minutes. Stir through the butter, if using. Portion up and cool completely before freezing, if not using immediately.

> Serves 8
> –
> Prep 5 mins
> –
> Cook 20 mins

CHEESE AND POPPYSEED BISCUITS

A pre-prepared roll of this in the freezer is a gift to your future self. Popping a few rounds of these in the oven to bridge the gap between getting home and dinnertime, or an after-school snack (my little boy likens them to Mini Cheddars!) is a complete time-saver. Cheesy, buttery and delicious warm, they're a great savoury snack or addition to a packed lunch.

160g (5½oz) salted butter, at room temperature
110g (3¾oz) parmesan, finely grated
50g (2oz) gruyère, finely grated
flaky sea salt and freshly ground black pepper
200g (7oz) plain (all-purpose) flour, sifted
½ tsp baking powder
30g (1oz) poppy seeds

Put the butter, cheeses, a generous pinch of flaky salt and a good grind of black pepper into a bowl. Mix together with a wooden spoon or using the paddle attachment of a stand mixer. Slowly incorporate the flour and baking powder and bring together to form a stiffish dough. On a clean surface, roll the dough into a sausage approximately 25cm (10in) long. Place a double layer of cling film (plastic wrap) on the surface and scatter the poppy seeds across the length. Roll the cheese dough over it until the whole of the outside is coated. Discard any spare poppy seeds and then use the cling film to tightly wrap the dough. Freeze.

When ready to cook, preheat the oven to 200°C/180°C fan/ 400°F/Gas 6. Let the dough come to room temperature for 5 minutes, then slice into 1cm (½in) rounds using a sharp knife. Wrap and refreeze any remaining dough. Place on a baking parchment-lined baking sheet and cook for 13–14 minutes, until golden around the edges. Cool on the tray for 10 minutes before transferring to a wire rack.

Tip
To eat straight away, wrap in cling film and chill for 30 minutes before baking on a baking parchment-lined baking sheet in an oven preheated to 200°C/180°C fan/400°F/Gas 6 for 8–10 minutes.

Makes 20–25
–
Prep 10 mins, plus chilling
–
Cook 15 mins

Freezer Fillers

STICKY TOFFEE DATE CAKE

Having emergency pudding on demand is just the level of organization I'm into. By making this delicious loaf and freezing it in slices, all it takes is a reheat and a nice drizzle of sticky toffee sauce to so excellently hit that sweet spot. Topped with ice cream, I think it's perfect all year round.

200g (7oz) medjool dates, pitted and roughly chopped
1 tsp bicarbonate of soda (baking soda)
175g (6oz) salted butter
160g (5½oz) soft light brown sugar
160g (5½oz) black treacle (blackstrap molasses)
225g (8oz) self-raising (self-rising) flour
2 tsp ground ginger
1 tsp ground cinnamon
½ tsp mixed spice
100ml (scant ½ cup) whole milk
2 eggs, beaten
cream, to serve (optional)

For the sauce
250g (9oz) salted butter
250g (9oz) soft light brown sugar
300ml (1¼ cups) double (heavy) cream
pinch of sea salt flakes

Grease and line a 1.5kg (3lb 5oz) loaf tin with baking parchment. Preheat the oven to 180°C/160°C fan/350°F/Gas 4.

Add the dates and bicarbonate of soda to a bowl and cover with 100ml (scant ½ cup) of boiling water. Allow to sit for 10 minutes before puréeing with a stick blender.

Put the butter, sugar and treacle in a saucepan and place over a low heat to melt, gently stirring with a wooden spoon. Remove from the heat.

Combine the flour and spices in a large bowl and combine the milk and eggs in another bowl. Make a well in the centre of the flour and whisk in the melted butter mixture, followed by the milk mixture and the date purée. Combine using a balloon whisk, then spoon into the prepared tin.

Bake for 50–55 minutes until a skewer inserted into the cake comes out clean. Cool in the tin for 10 minutes before transferring to a wire rack to cool completely. When cool, cut into ten slices. Separate each slice with a small piece of baking parchment and freeze in a big plastic bag.

To make the sauce, put the butter and sugar into a saucepan and place over a low heat, stirring until the butter has melted and the sugar has dissolved. Bring to the boil and bubble away for 30 seconds before removing from the heat and adding the cream and salt flakes (carefully as the mixture might spit). Mix together, then transfer to sterilized jars (see page 132) – the mixture makes 650g (1lb 7oz). Cool to room temperature then refrigerate.

For on-demand comfort, preheat the oven to 165°C/150°C fan/325°F/Gas 3. Put a slice of sticky toffee cake per person into a heatproof dish. Top each with 3 tablespoons of caramel sauce and bake for 10–12 minutes, until warmed through and soaked with delicious caramel. Alternatively, microwave (in a microwave-safe bowl) for 2 minutes.

Serves 10
–
Prep 15 mins, plus chilling
–
Cook 1 hour

CHOCOLATE CHIP COOKIE DOUGH

Having a couple of rolls of cookie dough stored in your freezer is a fast-track solution to becoming host of the year. Whether for last-minute guests or satisfying that post-dinner sweet itch, it's so handy having some homemade dough ready to go. Once you've got to grips with the basic recipe, you could add in mini marshmallows or toffee chunks and see where you end up!

150g (5½oz) salted butter, softened
150g (5½oz) soft light brown sugar
100g (3½oz) granulated sugar
1 egg, beaten
270g (9½oz) plain (all-purpose) flour
1 tsp baking powder
1 tsp bicarbonate of soda (baking soda)
1 tsp vanilla extract
1 tsp salt
200g (7oz) chocolate chunks (I use a mix of plain and white)
sea salt flakes, to sprinkle

Use a wooden spoon or the paddle attachment of a stand mixer to combine the butter and sugars in a bowl. Add the egg and mix to combine. Sift in the flour, baking powder and bicarbonate, then add the vanilla, salt and chocolate chunks. Mix with a wooden spoon to bring together, then divide the dough and form into two sausages approximately 19–20cm (7½–8in) long and 5–6cm (2–2½in) wide. Double wrap in cling film (plastic wrap) or baking parchment and then freeze.

To bake, preheat the oven to 180°C/160°C fan/350°F/Gas 4. Use a sharp knife to cut the log into 1.5cm (½in) rounds and place on a baking sheet lined with baking parchment, spacing them about 5cm (2in) apart. Sprinkle with a little flaky sea salt and bake for 12 minutes, until golden around the edges and still a little pale in the middle. Cool on the tray for 10 minutes and then transfer to a wire rack (or just eat warm).

Tip

To eat straight away, chill the roll for 30 minutes before slicing as above, placing on a lined baking sheet and baking in an oven preheated to 180°C/160°C fan/350°F/Gas 4 for 8–10 minutes, or until golden brown.

Makes 22–24
–
Prep 10 mins, plus chilling
–
Cook 12 mins

BLACKBERRY AND APPLE CRUMBLE

Even though this still needs a relatively long bake, getting the prep out of the way removes the hard work and means that the minute you desperately need some crumble, you're good to go. If you've got friends over for dinner and suddenly there's talk of a sweet treat after, you can pop this in the oven and it'll be ready just as you find space in your dessert stomach. Voilà!

250g (9oz) salted butter at room temperature, diced
400g (14oz) plain (all-purpose) flour, plus 1½ tbsp
150g (5½oz) caster (superfine) sugar
70g (2½oz) demerara sugar
650g (1lb 7oz) cooking (baking) apples, such as bramley, peeled, cored and cut into rough 1.5cm (½in) chunks (peeled weight roughly 500g/1lb 2oz)
450g (1lb) blackberries
75g (2½oz) soft light brown sugar
cream, ice cream or custard, to serve

To make the crumble, in a large bowl, rub the butter into the flour in using the tips of your fingers, until you have a crumble-like texture. Stir through the caster and demerara sugars, then transfer to a freezer bag.

For the fruit filling, add the chopped apples, blackberries, 1½ tablespoons of plain flour and the soft light brown sugar to a bowl and mix together, coating all the fruit in the flour and sugar. Again, transfer to a freezer bag. Freeze both bags.

Preheat the oven to 200°C/180°C fan/400°F/Gas 6. Choose a suitable baking dish for the number of crumble portions you're preparing. Tip 125g (4½oz) of frozen fruit per person into the dish and top with 100g (3½oz) of crumble mix per person. Bake for 50 minutes, until the topping is golden and the filling is bubbling. Serve with cream, ice cream or custard.

Tip

To eat straight away, prepare as above before cooking in an oven preheated to 200°C/180°C fan/400°F/Gas 6 for 30–40 minutes, until bubbling and golden.

Serves 8
–
Prep 10 mins
–
Cook 50 mins

SCONES

Scones are such a brilliant thing to have in your freezer. They're relatively simple to make (even warranting a child's help if you have one to hand) and freeze perfectly – ready to produce with the arrival of unscheduled guests. They taste completely of summer but I assure you that they're just as perfect in the depths of winter.

700g (1lb 9oz) self-raising (self-rising) flour, plus extra for dusting
2 tsp baking powder
180g (61/3oz) salted butter, chilled and cut into small cubes
80g (2¾oz) caster (superfine) sugar
350ml (1½ cups) whole milk
1 tsp lemon juice
1 egg, beaten
clotted cream and jam (jelly) or lemon curd, to serve

Preheat the oven to 220°C/200°C fan/425°F/Gas 7. Line two large baking sheets with baking parchment.

Sift the flour and baking powder into a large bowl, then rub the butter in using the tips of your fingers, until you have a crumble-like texture. Stir through the sugar. Combine the milk and lemon juice in a jug and then pour it into the flour mixture, stirring with a butter knife to bring it together.

Tip the mixture on to a lightly floured worktop and pull together with your hands to make a smooth(ish) dough, turning it a few times to bring it all together. Divide it in half and set one half aside. Roll the dough to 2cm (¾in) thick and use a 6.5cm (2½in) fluted cutter (measure the width on the fluted end) to cut out as many scone shapes as possible. Re-roll to make the rest (you should have seven or eight in total from this batch). Brush with the beaten egg and bake for 12–14 minutes on the middle shelf of the oven, until golden.

While they bake, repeat with the second batch of dough.

Cool on a wire rack after baking, then freeze. When ready to eat, defrost first and then warm through for a few minutes in a hot oven. Serve with clotted cream and jam or lemon curd.

Makes 15–16
–
Prep 15 mins
–
Cook 25 mins

PRESERVES

The most saccharinely fragrant of chapters – this set
of recipes targets the sweet tooth! Saving space in your
fridge and freezer, this is your old-fashioned batch cooking
– jarring things up to see you through the winter. The end
result is all the better for being homemade.

peach &
Apricot jam

SEVILLE ORANGE MARMALADE

There is an obligation, every January, to make marmalade – when the beautifully imperfect, pock-marked Seville oranges arrive in our greengrocers and supermarkets. I've never in my life craved marmalade on toast, but I love making it – and I love the flavour of this marmalade (particularly when still warm). It has a sweet, tangy bitterness to it, but it has a light flavour that tastes like the mellow aroma of oranges.

700g (1lb 9oz) Seville oranges
1 lmedium–large lemon, thin-skinned and organic
1.4kg (3lb 1oz) cane sugar

Rinse and dry the oranges before cutting them in half. Juice them and remove the inner membrane (the fleshy, edible-looking part of the fruit). Put the juice in a large glass bowl and the membrane and pips in a separate bowl. Quarter the orange peel 'shells' and flatten, pith-side down. Slice the peel, as finely as you can, and add to the bowl of juice. Juice the lemon and add this to the rest of the fruit juice.

Place all the membranes and the juiced lemon shell in a food processor and pulp. Pop this, with all the citrus seeds, in a sterile piece of muslin and tie with natural twine. Add the filled muslin bag to the glass bowl of juice and rind, along with 1.7 litres (a generous 6 cups) of water. Cover and leave overnight (or a minimum of 3 hours and a maximum of 24).

Pour everything from the glass bowl into a thick-based preserving pan or stockpot. Heat very gently and when small bubbles begin to appear on the surface, simmer for 2 hours or until the volume has reduced by a third (using a marker on a wooden spoon as a measurement). When the liquid is reduced, remove the muslin bag and squeeze out all the juice, using a sieve and the back of a spoon (this liquid contains all your pectin which will help the marmalade to set).

Add the sugar to the pan and cook over a low heat, until the sugar is dissolved. If using a metal spoon you will be able to feel the granules dissolving. Turn the heat to high. When the mixture is boiling, it should look like an overflowing fizzy drink. Boil for 10–15 minutes from when it comes to the boil, or until it reaches setting point, or 106°C (223°F) on a jam thermometer.

Leave to sit for 10 minutes before pouring into sterilized jars. Meanwhile, sterilize your jars, My preferred method to sterilize glass jars is first to thoroughly wash them in soapy water. After, place the jars and their lids in an oven preheated to 180°C/160°C fan/350°F/Gas 4, and heat for 10 minutes. Carefully remove and let cool slightly on a clean tea towel before filling (while still warm).

Makes about 2kg (4lb 8oz)
–
Prep 20 mins, plus soaking
–
Cook 2½ hours

PLUM COMPÔTE

With a lower sugar content than jam (jelly), this compôte doesn't have such a long shelf-life, but it is also a lot less sweet than jam, and truer to the natural fruit. The addition of amaretto magics the plums into having an almond-like flavour. I love this layered up in a jam jar between yoghurt and granola for a portable breakfast, but it's also a great dessert option with custard and crumbled shortbread.

1.4kg (3lb 1oz) plums, quartered and stoned
juice of 2 lemons
300g (10½oz) granulated sugar
75ml (generous ¼ cup) amaretto, or water

Add all the ingredients to a large pan and bring to a simmer. Simmer for 30 minutes, until the fruit has broken down and is nicely juicy. Increase the heat to a boil and cook for 4–5 minutes, until slightly thickened. Allow to cool slightly before decanting into sterilized jars (see page 132). This will keep in the fridge for up to three weeks, or can be frozen in tubs or freezer bags.

Makes 1.6kg (3lb 8oz)
–
Prep 10 mins
–
Cook 40 mins

Preserves

VEGETABLE PICKLE

This is my humble response to the ever-delicious Branston pickle. To me, a homemade pickle or chutney has the added flavour of satisfaction! Chopping, simmering and jarring makes this taste extra good – and paired with cheese and apple in a ploughman's lunch, it's a store-cupboard gift that will keep giving.

2 onions, roughly chopped
250ml (generous 1 cup) cider vinegar
550g (1lb 3oz) cooking (baking) apples, peeled, cored and cut into 1.5cm (½in) cubes
2 tomatoes, roughly chopped
200g (7oz) soft dark brown sugar
2 tbsp tomato purée (paste)
100g (3½oz) medjool dates, pitted and roughly chopped
2 tbsp tamarind paste
½ tsp garlic powder
½ swede (rutabaga) (about 350g/12oz), peeled and cut into 0.5cm (¼in) cubes
4 carrots (350g/12oz), peeled and cut into 0.5cm (¼in) cubes

Add the onions, vinegar, apples, tomatoes, sugar, tomato purée, dates, tamarind paste and garlic powder to a heavy-based pan. Place over a low–medium heat to simmer and then bubble, until the apple is softened and the mixture is thick (40–45 minutes).

Meanwhile, bring a pan of salted water to the boil and add the swede. Cook for 5 minutes before adding the carrots and cooking for a further 4 minutes. Drain and add to a bowl of iced water to cool completely. Drain, then stir through the finished chutney. Spoon into sterilized jars (see page 132).

Makes 1.4kg
(3lb 1oz)
–
Prep 20 mins
–
Cook 45 mins

RHUBARB AND GINGER JAM

I love the process of making jam (jelly) – the slow ritual of the prep followed by the puckering bubble of the boil, and then a reward that can sit in the store cupboard for months. Some people like to use jam sugar or add pectin to their rhubarb jam (because rhubarb is naturally very low in pectin, which is what traditionally sets jam) but I love this concoction being a soft set. It's perfect spooned through yoghurt, or oozed onto crumpets.

1kg (2lb 2oz) trimmed rhubarb, chopped into 2–3cm (¾–1¼in) lengths
1kg (2lb 2oz) granulated sugar
juice of 2 lemons
200g (7oz) stem (preserved) ginger balls, finely chopped

Put the ingredients in a bowl and mix to combine. Cover and set aside for 2 hours.

After 2 hours, the rhubarb should have started to release some lovely juices. Spoon the mixture into a heavy-based preserving pan or stockpot. Place over a low heat until the sugar has all dissolved – this should take about 10 minutes. Bring to the boil and bubble for another 10 minutes until it reaches 106°C (223°F) on a sugar thermometer. Let it sit for 10 minutes, then ladle into sterilized jars (see page 132).

Makes approx.
1.8kg (4lb)
–
Prep 10 mins,
plus macerating
–
Cook 20 min

PEACH AND APRICOT JAM

This jam (jelly) is an ideal way to capture the season of delicious, ripe peaches. By adding dried apricots, there are little pops of more concentrated flavour, all in a sweet, amber coating. Obviously delicious on toast, try this spooned through a combination of Greek yoghurt and lightly whisked double (heavy) cream, scattered with crushed amaretti biscuits.

1.5kg (3lb 5oz) ripe but firm peaches (approx. 10), stoned and roughly chopped
500g (1lb 2oz) ready-to-eat dried apricots, roughly chopped
juice of 2 lemons
1.2kg (2lb 10oz) granulated sugar

Add the peaches, apricots and lemon juice to a large, heavy-based pan and place over a low heat for about 15 minutes, until the peaches are softening and juicy (you can encourage them by lightly mashing with the back of a spoon, if you like). Add the sugar and heat, stirring every now and then, until dissolved (about 6–7 minutes). Increase the heat and bring to the boil. Bubble away for 10–12 minutes, or until the mixture reaches 104°C (219°F), stirring every now and then to stop it from catching.

Meanwhile, sterilize your jars as per the instructions on page 132.

When the jam has reached setting point (see tip, below), turn off the heat and allow it to cool slightly so the mixture can thicken (this will help the fruit to distribute more evenly). Use a spoon to scrape any scum from the top of the pan and discard. Ladle the jam into the jars. Store in a cool, dark place and refrigerate once opened.

Tip
To test whether a jam has reached its setting point, put a spoonful on a cold plate and place in the fridge for 2 minutes. Draw your finger through the jam, and if it wrinkles then setting point has been reached. If not, continue to heat then test again.

Makes 2.5kg
(5lb 8oz)
–
Prep 10 mins
–
Cook 30 mins

INDEX

a

almonds
  chicken korma 76
  red pepper, almond and
    pecorino soup 41
  white gazpacho 98
apples
  blackberry and apple
    crumble 126
  vegetable pickle 136
apricots: peach and apricot
  jam 141
asparagus: pea and asparagus
  orzotto 97

b

bacon
  loaded potato skins 54
  macaroni cheese 59
baked beans 70
basil: fresh pesto 104
beans
  baked beans 70
  butter beans with kale and
    pancetta 72
  chilli con carne 15
beef
  beef shin ragù 9
  Bolognaise 13
  lasagne 11
  massaman curry 75
  meatballs 92
  sticky short ribs 80
beetroot soup 44
biscuits
  cheese and poppy-seed
    biscuits 121
  chocolate chip cookie dough
    124
blackberry and apple crumble
  126
Bolognaise 13
  chilli con carne 15
bread
  garlic bread 114
  salmorejo 100
  white gazpacho 98
breadcrumbs
  cheese and ham croquettes
    110

macaroni cheese 59
meatballs 92
salmon fishcakes 113
butter beans with kale and
  pancetta 72

c

cake, sticky toffee date 122
caponata 66
caramelized onion chutney:
  sausage rolls 117
cauliflower: chickpea and
  cauliflower curry 68
cheese
  butter beans with kale and
    pancetta 72
  cheese and ham croquettes
    110
  cheese and poppy-seed
    biscuits 121
  courgette and feta soup with
    fresh pesto 104
  fish pie 48
  fresh pesto 104
  lasagne 11
  leek and Camembert risotto
    107
  loaded potato skins 54
  macaroni cheese 59
  meatballs 92
  moussaka 56
  mushroom soup 34
  pea and asparagus orzotto
    97
  red pepper, almond and
    pecorino soup 41
  squash and goats' cheese
    quiche 23
  tuna sweetcorn pasta bake
    61
chicken
  chicken and mushroom pie
    27
  chicken and mushrooms 24
  chicken korma 76
  chicken ramen 18
  chicken thighs with dates
    and olives 53
  chicken with chorizo and
    tomatoes 84

roast chicken with lemon,
  olives and new potatoes 16
chickpeas
  chickpea and cauliflower
    curry 68
  chickpea and lentil soup 43
chilli con carne 15
chocolate chip cookie dough
  124
chorizo: chicken with chorizo
  and tomatoes 84
cider: pulled pork 87
coconut milk
  massaman curry 75
  sweet potato and spinach
    dhal 64
  Thai-style spiced butternut
    squash soup 30
compôte, plum 135
cookie dough, chocolate chip
  124
courgettes (zucchini)
  courgette and feta soup with
    fresh pesto 104
  roasted vegetables 50
cream
  scones 128
  sticky toffee date cake 122
  tomato soup 33
cream cheese
  fish pie 48
  pea and asparagus orzotto
    97
creamy onion soup 39
croquettes, cheese and ham
  110
crumble, blackberry and apple
  126
cucumber, pickled 80
  curry
  chicken korma 76
  chickpea and cauliflower
    curry 68
  massaman curry 75
  sweet potato and spinach
    dhal 64
  Thai-style spiced butternut
    squash soup 30

d

date cake, sticky toffee 122

dhal, sweet potato and
spinach 64
dressing, tahini 20

e
equipment 5

f
fennel: sausage and fennel
ragù 89
fish
fish pie 48
kedgeree 102
salmon fishcakes 113
salmorejo 100
tuna sweetcorn pasta bake
61
freezing food 4–5

g
gazpacho, white 98
ginger
chicken korma 76
rhubarb and ginger jam 138
sticky short ribs 80

h
ham: cheese and ham
croquettes 110
hoisin sauce: sticky short ribs
80

j
jam (jelly)
peach and apricot jam 141
rhubarb and ginger jam 138
scones 128
jars, sterilizing 132

k
kedgeree 104
korma, chicken 76

l
lamb
moussaka 56
spiced Middle Eastern-style
lamb shoulder 91
lasagne 11
leek and Camembert risotto
107

lemons
roast chicken with lemon,
olives and new potatoes 16
spiced Middle Eastern-style
lamb shoulder 91
lentils
chickpea and lentil soup 43
sweet potato and spinach
dhal 64
loaded potato skins 54

m
macaroni cheese 59
marmalade, Seville orange 132
massaman curry 75
meatballs 92
minestrone 36
moussaka 56
mushrooms
chicken and mushroom pie
27
chicken and mushrooms 24
chicken ramen 18
mushroom soup 34
mustard: sausage rolls 117

n
noodles: chicken ramen 18

o
olives
caponata 66
chicken thighs with dates
and olives 53
roast chicken with lemon,
olives and new potatoes 16
onions: creamy onion soup 39
oranges: Seville orange
marmalade 132
orzo: pea and asparagus
orzotto 97

p
pancetta, butter beans with
kale and 72
peach and apricot jam 141
pea and asparagus orzotto 97
pesto, courgette and feta soup
with fresh 104
pickles

pickled cucumber 80
vegetable pickle 136
pies
chicken and mushroom pie
27
fish pie 48
plum compôte 135
poppy seeds: cheese and
poppy seed biscuits 121
pork
meatballs 92
pulled pork 87
sweet and sour pork 82
potatoes: loaded potato skins
54
prawns (shrimp)
fish pie 48
kedgeree 102
pulled pork 87

q
quiche, squash and goats'
cheese 23

r
ragù
beef shin ragù 9
lasagne 11
sausage and fennel ragù 89
ramen, chicken 18
reheating food 4
rhubarb and ginger jam 138
risotto, leek and Camembert
107

s
salmorejo 100
sausage rolls 117
sausage and fennel ragù 89
scones 128
Seville orange marmalade 132
spaghetti: meatballs 92
spiced Middle Eastern-style
lamb shoulder 91
squash
roasted squash with tahini
and herbs 20
squash and goats' cheese
quiche 23

Thai-style spiced butternut
squash soup 30
sticky short ribs 80
sticky toffee date cake 122
sweet and sour pork 82
sweet potato and spinach
dhal 64
sweetcorn: tuna sweetcorn
pasta bake 61

t
tahini: roasted squash with
tahini and herbs 20
Thai-style spiced butternut
squash soup 30
toffee: sticky toffee date cake
122

tomato sauce 118
meatballs 92
tuna sweetcorn pasta bake 61

v
vegetables
roasted vegetables 50
vegetable pickle 136

w
white gazpacho 98
white wine: leek and
Camembert risotto 107

ACKNOWLEDGEMENTS

There is so much love and effort that goes into the creation of a book, and never have I been so acutely aware of that than in the making of this! Just as these recipes are predominantly family-style, it felt like a family helped to build and bind this, on many levels.

My first thanks to Sofie Shearman, for the opportunity and the leeway! Sofie – you're the most patient and kind editor, simultaneously meticulous and thoughtful, while allowing your teams the creative license that energizes them. You made the whole process a joy and made my segue into maternity leave seamless.

Rita – hilarious and gorgeous. Each shoot day felt like a treat, and the photography is perfection. Thank you for the moral support since day dot! Max – your prop game is on fire. You made every set-up a dream, and all the food as appetizing as I could ever hope. Thanks, as always, for just being a general star. Katy Everett, the designer extraordinaire pulling it all together. Thank you for your cool and calm energy, and willingness to house leftovers.

This job would be impossible without my assistants – the best company and the most capable chefs. Shooting this book till I was 36 weeks pregnant, you all picked up extra slack (literally lugging the shopping where I couldn't), and I'm so grateful for your competence. Thanks for always humouring me – Jess, Maria and Caitlin.

Mum and Dad – I have you to thank for teaching me how to cook for a crowd, a skill I have taken into adult life. I think everyone should know the definition of 'bowl food'. Even now, you've not blinked at having four extra mouths to feed for our extended stay, and we all love you for it!

Justin, your positivity and can-do attitude is infectious. The foot-rubs, back-rubs and hype talks kept me going. Ted – thanks for never noticing how often you had to eat tuna pasta bake to get through eight adult portions. And Maggie – thanks for an easy(ish) ride, and for giving me the time to edit!